School of t...

MW00810958

School

OF THE

Elemental Beings

—⁓—

Karsten Massei

—⁓—

with illustrations by

Franziska von der Geest

SteinerBooks | 2017

Copyright © 2017 by SteinerBooks | Anthroposophic Press

Published by
SteinerBooks | Anthroposophic Press
610 Main Street
Great Barrington, Massachusetts 01230

www.steinerbooks.org

  print ISBN: 978-1-62148-145-4
e-book ISBN: 978-1-62148-146-1

This work was originally published as *Schule der Elementarwesen* by Futurum Verlag, Basel, 2011.

Translated from the German by Monica Gold

Printed in the United States of America

~w~ CONTENTS ~w~

V. Caring for the Earth

VI. Verses of Blessing

Translator's Note

After reading this book in its original German, I felt an urgency that it should become available in English, especially for young people, including my grandchildren.
With all my heart I thank Giselher Weber for advice and help, but especially for his editing skills.

—Monica Gold

INTRODUCTION

IN THIS BOOK will be found information about facts that cannot be perceived with ordinary sense perception, because descriptions will be given of beings of the elemental world and their living conditions. These elemental beings do not exist for ordinary sense organs, because these beings do not penetrate into the world that offers itself to these senses. But even if they remain invisible to sensory contemplation, these beings are recognizable through what they produce. What they produce does not hide itself from sensory perception. On the contrary, everything a human being perceives around him or her is produced through the activity and existence of elemental beings. Every water drop, every blossom, every leaf, every gust of wind, every light, every perceivable form has as its basis the existence and the activity of elemental beings. Their works appear to human senses although they themselves remain hidden behind these works. They disappear into what they bring about. They lose themselves into the work that arises through them.

Information will be given for people who are accustomed to regarding what is sensory as the only reality, which will seem to them unbelievable and fantastic. To our intellect, which has been schooled only for the sense world, the world that opens beyond it must appear in this way. That is unavoidable. And yet it is important to familiarize oneself with information that reports about this other invisible world, because it does at least expand our view of sensory reality.

Generally, we hear of these beings of the elemental world as gnomes, nymphs (undines), sylphs, and fairies. They have their firm place in fairy tales and myths of all peoples. There they appear as spirits that test human beings and support them in their development. They also appear as warning and serving spirits. They help us, yet they also challenge us. This shows that they have a wisdom about life at their disposal, in which they are superior to human beings. They approach us while following, in their actions, laws of life of a higher order. They embody something that humans have not yet integrated into themselves, something we still have to learn to bring into reality through our existence.

This old folk knowledge about how elemental beings and nature spirits actually form a world with the human being has survived many centuries in numerous fairy tales and folk sagas. Therefore, even today one can get to know elemental beings through fairy tales if one reads them as true stories—for fairy tales are still taking place. They are not stories that merely belong to the past. On the contrary, the truths portrayed in fairy tales have timeless value and importance. When we come into contact with elemental beings, we will again and again have the experience that we recognize descriptions like those appearing in fairy tales. They originate wherever our human souls become interested in what speaks to us out of nature.

There exists something like a fairy tale sphere of the earth and of life. It is actually the life sphere in which the elemental beings live. To get to know it is like a journey on which one encounters fairy tales that are quite real.

From a general point of view it can be said that the elemental beings form the life organism of the earth. Through them the cosmic impulses are gathered that make the earth into a living organism. Indeed, one can experience the elemental world as a large living vessel in which spiritual impulses of higher beings are collected. These impulses must be accepted by the earth and its beings; otherwise they could not unfold their effectiveness. This is precisely the task of the beings of the elemental world. They absorb cosmic life impulses and through their existence bring them into reality in earthly connection. They live out of these cosmic impulses that make the earth into a living organism.

Therefore, it might not be surprising that among the elementals there are many beings with an astonishing intelligence and wisdom. Their intelligence, however, serves the life of the earth. Through them the earth conditions are created. When we observe nature with our senses, we look at the testimony of the intelligence of elemental beings. In the manifold observable forms and colors, the living shapes of plants and animals, the color manifestations of the sky, in the entirety of sense-perceptible life, their intelligence appears to the senses of the human being. The elemental beings are the beings through which wisdom in nature becomes effective. They are the embodiment, the bearers of this wisdom.

This nature intelligence has an effect on us through our senses. By meeting nature we inevitably meet this nature intelligence. We live in the weaving of nature, which is imbued with cosmic wisdom—we are just not always conscious of this fact. This is just as well, because we have other tasks than to enjoy exclusively the pleasures of nature. Yet we are being sustained and nourished by the nature surrounding us. We are dependent on this nature for sustaining us and our life. As we have seen, precisely the elemental beings bear the task to form the earthly world. They offer to humans what we find as our living space. That is the space in which we lead our life, and through which we gain possibilities to develop ourselves. Therefore, the elemental beings justifiably say, "You, human being, are our guest." The elemental beings indeed see themselves as hosts of the human beings on earth. They consider human beings to be superior to them; through our capacities we are above them, and yet they serve us in our development. Through them we human beings receive our right to hospitality on the earth. It is their life, their life's impulses, their existence to which we owe our own life and development.

To come into contact with elemental beings, it can be helpful to dedicate oneself intensively to the phenomena of the sense world. It is really a wish of the elemental beings that human beings would pay enough attention to the sense world. The elementals live as spiritual beings in the physical world; they penetrate it, enliven it, and are completely bound up in the observable transformational occurrences. This surface of existence that can be experienced through the senses will always contain possibilities through which we can find access to the beings of the elemental world. In this way a profound sensory experience can definitely lead to a meeting with the elemental beings. Through colors, forms, the consistency of substances, and the gestures of living beings, one can gain insights into the working activity of the elemental beings. The structure of the bark of a tree; the scent of a landscape in the morning; the silence of a mountain; the rushing of waves; the sound of a stone; all these can guide us to experiences that give us an idea of the living working activity of the elemental beings.

From this experience an astonishment, a wonder can arise that has a cognitive character. In fact, while we experience such wonder, our souls may connect so strongly with our own life's surroundings that the veil of the sense world can be lifted. Our souls are being touched inwardly by the world in which the elemental beings live. This occurs because our astonishment causes a transformational process among the elementals. They experience the soul of an astonished human being, and through this they feel recognized. Astonishment, but also intensified perceiving, is a gift for them from a human being. By this they are oriented. Elemental beings receive an orientation from the feelings of astonishment, attention, and also the gratitude of humans. Through this the elementals find their way to a center to which nothing else can lead them, including any higher spiritual being. Human beings have the possibility to increase the fullness of life for the beings of the elemental world. We can do it by connecting awakened senses and purified feelings with nature and its phenomena. When we do this, we give or work from the heart, and this is experienced by the elemental beings. For them, this increase of the fullness of life through humanity is extremely important. Under no circumstances should one underestimate the importance that a human being has for the beings of the elemental world. The elemental beings want to be carried in the hearts of human beings. They would like to find their orientation through human beings, and yearn for humans who accomplish this work of the heart. Gaining knowledge about the connection that exists between human beings and the elemental beings could become one's own separate, important field of research. The purpose of this book is to contribute to such research.

One can have the surprising experience of coming into contact with spiritual beings from the elemental world who want to work together with the human being. We can designate such beings as the higher beings of the elemental world. They are destined to connect themselves deeply with the world of humans, and have the wish to do so. House spirits belong to this group of beings, as do tree spirits, and certain elemental beings of the landscape. They come toward a human being by spiritually standing by his or her side. They support him or her by accepting the questions and leading where he or she wishes to be led. This book will report in detail about these higher elemental beings that are closely connected with humanity. They repeatedly met me on my own path and have also supported my work on this book.

Above all, they are to be described and allowed to speak for themselves.

Meeting a human being who gives them his or her attention and time means the greatest happiness for these elevated elemental beings. I have met many such beings in the most diverse places. I have experienced their astonishment and their happiness about a human being who turns toward them. Again and again I have heard them say, "You come to us, take the time, and do not go; you linger, and you give a gift to us from the precious timespan of your life."

I.
THE WORLD OF THE ELEMENTAL BEINGS

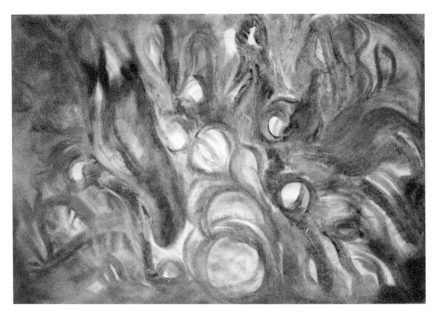

The Seed of the Earth

What Are Elemental Beings?

Where do elemental beings live? How do they live? What imagination can one make of them? How can we come into contact with them?

Beings of the elemental world, or nature spirits, cannot be perceived with the normal senses. One cannot see them. Also one cannot taste or feel them; similarly one cannot hear them as one hears a sound or a voice. In spite of this, they constantly surround the human being. They live in things and in living beings that human beings can perceive with their senses. Elemental beings live in plants, in animals we can see; they live in the water, in the air, in light, and in warmth. And they live in the earth. They live in all elements. Every leaf, every blossom, every water drop, every stone, every piece of wood, every metal; yes, every substance is penetrated with beings of the elemental world.

Yet if an inner sense for elementals has been awakened, one can also observe them in nature. One can discover them at forest creeks, on roots of large trees, in flower gardens, at the edges of forests or in the reeds. They live with people in their houses. Also in cities one can observe a great number of highly evolved beings of the elemental world; they are very important for the social life of people. Even in machines and technical appliances, one can meet them.

There is also a large group of wandering elemental beings. I have been fortunate to make acquaintance with many of them. They are very fond of human beings, for they share our destiny of being able to move over the earth. From time to time they stop and remain with a person or group of people. Then they continue their journey.

There are also elemental beings who accompany human beings. They like to listen to human beings and enjoy being carried around by them. But such beings are obliged to remain quiet and unobtrusive so long as we ourselves do not begin to turn to them of our own volition. It is the task of these beings to be silent companions of human beings and their development. They wait for human beings.

The Ordering of Elemental Beings

Elemental beings exist in a hierarchical order; their relationships among one another are strictly ordered. The principle of life itself expresses itself in this order of the elemental beings. Every elemental being has its own tasks, which are given to it. It cannot deviate from its given path. Life on earth as we know it can continue to exist only because the elemental beings are woven into its order. If this were not so, if only a few of them were to deviate from the tasks given to them by higher beings, life on earth would lose its coherence. The human being would lose the stability that he or she needs to be able to develop.

The beings of the elemental world live in an order that is different from the beings of the physical world. They do not live beside each other, but rather they live a life in which they mutually penetrate each other. One being is always a life-sheath for a number of other beings. Normally, more highly evolved beings provide a mantle of life for lower ones. So, for example, a tree spirit lives in a tree; but it is also a being in which a large number of other very differentiated elemental beings live. These elemental beings live their lives in the spirit of the tree. They can be active for the tree only because they are part of the being of the tree. The innumerable beings of the leaves; the blossoms; beings of the bark; the large and tiny wood spirits; the guardians of the buds;

the guardians of the seeds—all these are not capable of connecting themselves with the physical tree on their own. This connection becomes possible for them only because they integrate themselves into the spirit of the tree. They live in the being of the tree spirit, so that they can fulfill their tasks for the tree. This principle (that the higher spirits provide the sheath of life for the lower ones) can often be found in the realm of elemental beings. The lesser spirits are part of the greater spirits. The greater ones make themselves available so that the lesser ones can live and become active through them.

It can also occur, however, that higher spirits live within lower ones. In trees, this may happen when higher spirits enter into certain trees. Trees standing in special places often provide living spaces for beings who take on tasks for the surrounding landscape. In certain trees one can find beings that rank higher than the individual tree spirit. In spite of this, the higher ones subordinate themselves to the tree spirit. They adapt themselves to the being of the tree spirit by slipping into it. In this way they are able to become active in the larger surrounding landscape.

The forces with which the individual beings of the elemental world associate and become active assign them to their position in the hierarchy of the elementals. The higher the forces that a being is working with and that it has to manage, the higher its hierarchical position. This hierarchical order of the elemental beings is an important characteristic of their nature. The world of life of the earth, the etheric world, is structured and ordered based on this principle.

Elemental Beings of Higher and Lower Rank

On one hand, elemental beings are differentiated through the element to which they belong; on the other hand, they are also differentiated through the realm of nature to which they are attached. Elementals are very different beings depending on whether they belong to the realm of plants, of animals, or of human beings. Elemental beings are further differentiated by how deeply they are connected with the fundamental processes in nature. There are elemental beings that devote themselves fully to the processes of substances. These beings have hardly what we would call a life of their own; they merge totally with what they have given themselves to. There are an incalculable number of these beings. Wherever there are fundamental processes taking place, elemental beings of this kind are living. It is justified to say that they belong to the lower ranks of elemental beings because they are bound to processes of substance formation. Above them stand beings who are less bound to substance formation. The higher one rises in the ranks of the elemental beings, the freer the beings are from the processes of substance formation. Instead they exhibit more and more what one can describe as a life of their own.

Finally, one meets beings who live in a particular community with human beings. On the one hand, these higher elemental beings are bound through their tasks to whatever occurs generally in nature. On the other hand, because of their stage of development, they are in a position to draw closer to human beings. They are able to meet us, and can even initiate such meetings on their own. They can go toward a human being and show themselves. It is a question of our presence of mind, of attentiveness on our side whether we notice such a being. This fact is of great importance. Quite a bit depends on whether people take notice of these meetings. My observations repeatedly confirm that human beings are at all times surrounded by many elemental beings. Wherever we are, they are there to observe us. They live literally everywhere. And they wish for human beings to acquire a sense of their presence.

Many of these highly evolved elemental beings recognize whether, and to what degree, human beings are unfree. They see if an individual life follows a set pattern. They acquired this ability to see because they themselves, through their own development, have been able to detach themselves from being bound to nature forces. They know what it means to be bound and to lend one's life to a foreign power. For this reason they recognize the patterns in which human beings think and bind themselves. It is their wish that human beings recognize their constraints and overcome them. Elementals want to go into the future with free human beings. For this reason they entreat the human being. They try to get human beings to recognize and pay attention to the spiritual life of the earth. They wish that human beings would recognize the position that the human being holds in relation to nature and the development of the earth. And they also wish that we human beings would recognize ourselves for who we really are.

To approach nature, to feel into it, means to meet the spiritual beings who are sisters and brothers of the human beings on the earth. They serve us, and we can serve them. To recognize the connections in which the human being lives with the earth and its beings means to accept the laws that determine the overall development of the earth and the human being. In this sense, the more highly evolved elemental beings stand by the side of human beings and accompany them. They whisper to us:

Walk
 Slowly
Your own steps
 Out of you shall arise
The life
 Of your soul

Fall
    And do not fall
Fall correctly
According to the ability of your soul
    Then we hold you
    [We] do not hold you
    And you notice
    Or [we] push you
    And you notice
When it comes from us
From the beings
Of the living earth.

The Birth of Elemental Beings

Elemental beings appear within earthly conditions of space and time. An elemental being appears at a particular time at a certain place, separating out of the astral kingdom beyond time and space, and entering into the etheric realm of the earth. Thus elemental beings are born. Suprasensory observation shows that this birth occurs for the various elemental beings in different, unique ways.

The spirits that live in the earth, the gnomes, come out of the earth. Their astral home is in the interior of the earth; out of this they arise. They are being born out of the interior spiritual light of the earth and rise to the surface through the various spiritual layers of the earth. The special intelligence of gnomes is connected with their origin. In certain areas they are equal to a human, or even superior, because on their way before birth they traverse the spiritual strata of the earth. In comparison to the other elemental beings, they stand closest to the human being because they themselves have become most strongly penetrated by the character of the earth.

Gnomes that rise to the surface of the earth often enter earthly living conditions through hollows. Such birth-hollows can be found among roots of old tree trunks. These birth-hollows are sacred places. Not all hollows are birth-hollows, but one can find them now and again. The gnomes say that such a hollow is a womb of the earth.

The spirits of the water, or nymphs (also called undines) have their birthplaces where the earth element mixes with the element of water. Wherever water and earth penetrate each other in a living way at the bottom of lakes and rivers, one can find these places. The water beings do not rise from the earth as the gnomes do. Both earth and water are necessary, so that life-germs can be created from which the nymphs arise. The places that lodge and shelter the life-germs of the nymphs are protected by special beings. These beings are of a sublime nature, filled with kindness and goodness, and therefore stand in a living relationship to the beings of the higher hierarchies. One can call these beings the "mothers" of the water. They are very withdrawn beings. Like many higher elemental beings, they distinguish themselves by almost completely disappearing behind the task that they fulfill. Especially because they remain in the background they are not easily perceived. They do not want to be disturbed by human beings; their work is far too important and meaningful for the earth.

Spirits of the air, or sylphs, are born in yet a different way. Wherever water mixes with light and air, spiritual spaces open out of which sylphs emerge. Foaming, splashing water from mountain streams and waterfalls offers the preconditions for beings of air to be born. Light is necessary for their birth. Clouds that push their way in front of the sun interrupt the arising of the sylphs. Only when the sun shines again into the foaming water do the young sylphs or sylph children come forth. Air beings can also be born in a different way. Where light and warmth penetrate the air, places arise where sylphs can come forth. These places are in the air itself. They are small spiritual gates through which the young sylphs cross over from the astral world into the etheric.

The birth of warmth beings happens in the warmth. For this to take place, no other element is required. The elemental beings who are the carriers of the element of warmth are born out of the warmth itself.

It can be observed suprasensibly that the birth of an elemental being is accompanied by a dying process. When a gnome is being born, the light-germ is extinguished that had arisen from the depths of the earth. When a nymph emerges, an earth being that gave itself to aid the birth of the nymph sinks into the earth. This earth being forms the dying sheath of the water being that appears. So that a sylph can be born, a water being sacrifices itself and disappears in the splashing water. Only for the birth of a warmth being is it not necessary for another elemental being of a different element to pass away. The reason for this is that warmth is an immediate expression of the spiritual, the realm of ideas. The creative force of ideas lives in the warmth. The birth of the warmth being is, therefore, not dependent on the sacrifice of other elemental beings.

Life Cycles of the Beings of the Elemental World

Elemental beings experience various conditions of life. In connection with the earth, one can say that sometimes they sleep more, yet at other times they are more awake. When they sleep in relation to the earth, they have entered a condition of enchantment. They are bound into the physical conditions of the earth. The leaf being is then in the leaf. The beings that live in the frozen water of a lake are enchanted.

When a storm arises, definite air beings are captured in it. They are released only when the storm subsides. Rain tempts certain water beings to appear; drought lets them disappear, yet it awakens in them the longing to be enchanted again into the matter of water. For the elemental beings, to be enchanted into earthly conditions means to sleep. As they disengage from these conditions, they awaken from their earthly sleep.

Elemental beings are also connected with the physical makeup of the earth. However, their bond is not so strong that one could say that they have a physical body like human beings. One can more correctly say that they dissolve themselves into matter. They go right into matter. For them, this slipping into matter means that they subordinate themselves completely to the conditions and necessities of the earth. They fall asleep as they enter into earthly conditions. Only as sleeping spirits can they fully give themselves to their work and tasks. One can say that they fall into a stupor, and only in this way can they serve higher beings in the service of which they stand with their tasks. Of course, not all beings of the various elements are dull like this. The gnomes are indeed wide awake, although they are enchanted into matter. Their ability consists of being especially awake and spiritually present. It is different with the water spirits; they can fulfill their tasks only because they dream. Through this they bear the laws of life into conditions essential for life. These laws of life originate in a world that is of a higher order than the physical. They originate in the astral world.

As soon as elemental beings free themselves from their enchantment, they leave the physical world. They separate from the earth and enter their spiritual home, the astral world. For the physical world, this generally means that substances lose their cohesion. Leaves wilt, fruit decays, wood crumbles. Also, when stones are broken, the elemental beings become detached from the stone in which they lived.

In avalanches and rockslides this occurs on a large scale. Also the felling of trees means that certain beings are freed from their enchantment. In burning matter the same occurs.

When one follows elemental beings with spiritual perception, one can observe that after they are released from their enchantment, they are received by the spiritual beings from which they originated. They rise through this transformation from the etheric to the astral world. They can then be seen only when a person has the ability to see in the astral world. Otherwise they are lost from sight.

These elemental beings are received and protected in the astral world by beings that belong to a higher dimension. They ascend into a world that is inhabited by beings purely spiritual in nature. They are now fully pulled out of physical conditions. The beings of the elemental world form a living bridge between the astral world and the life conditions of the physical world.

When conditions on earth arise once more for which a particular elemental being is needed, it will again descend from the astral world. The beings that protected it let it go free. In the astral world the seed essence is prepared so that it can be reborn into earth conditions. The elemental being enters again into enchantment and connects itself with its earthly tasks.

A Path to Elemental Beings

When one takes on the task to research the world that is closed to physical senses, one will be confronted with events that can be understood only gradually. Step by step, one has to come to know this world, which has its own laws. One will be confronted by connections or contexts that one cannot at first accept as possible. For this reason especially, the faculty of accurate observation is a prerequisite for understanding the spiritual world—as it is for the sense world. Achieving accurate observations and perceptions in the spiritual world is a path of soul development. Clear and unclouded perception is a prerequisite for a deeper understanding of the connections in the spiritual world.

When one would like to research the facts of a situation, it is never beneficial to limit the perceptions that could be made about it. To begin with, one perception is never more important than another. Every perception is significant; and in each perception something is hidden that wants to be communicated to the human being. This principle is valid both for the sense world and for the spiritual world. Every phenomenon speaks; and in every one a part of the whole truth can be found.

Suprasensory experiences can arise quite spontaneously in the human soul. For a brief moment the veil of the senses tears open, and a perception of the world that lies behind the veil takes hold of the soul. I believe that every human being who researches the past will remember such experiences. Strictly speaking, every thought and every memory is a suprasensory event that takes place in the human soul; but in most cases these occurrences proceed subconsciously.

Deliberate perception in the spiritual world normally requires schooling. Spontaneous, sudden insights do not give the soul the satisfaction it wants. The reason is that sudden insights do not provide certainty about the inner nature of the beings of the spiritual world. The wish or the need to recognize the world and its beings that conceal themselves behind the veil of senses requires that one find suitable methods to learn suprasensible perception.

I do not want to keep it a secret that three remarkable personalities were very important for me on this path of schooling. Those are Rudolf Steiner, Emma Kunz, and Edward Bach. I owe a great deal to the works of these spiritual scientists. Without them this book would not have been written.

All three undertook an intensive path of self-education, and have left us much testimonial evidence of their paths. Again and again I have looked for answers in their works.

An important question stood at the beginning of my own research. It was a question about the healing effects of plants. I studied many books, but began to mistrust certain indications, as I noticed that individual authors copied from each other. This discovery created a wish in me to do my own research. I began to ascertain the effects of plants, by taking their organs—blossoms, leaves and roots—into my own hands, attentively observing what happened in me as a result. I continued this study for many months and documented all results meticulously. Through this intensive work I gained the faculty of observing accurately the reaction of my own body to certain substances. I experienced both healing influences and the poisonous effects of plants, and I compared them with descriptions in various books. During this time I took a course in the preparation of flower essences according to Edward Bach. In the following three years I myself produced a series of flower essences. I was especially interested to understand how the process of creating flower essences can be explained spiritually. Through the exact observation of procedures with delicate material, the faculty for perceiving the elemental world began to intensify in me. I could observe that the essences come about thanks to the help and support of beings from the elemental world. These beings mediate between the spiritual plant being and the physical carrier substance, water.

The trees also gave me the possibility to refine my perceiving skills. I don't know how much time I spent with them. One winter stands out in my memory, when I visited certain trees, daily whenever possible. I leaned against their trunks and lived into their being. With time, I learned to differentiate successfully between the various qualities of the trees. I compared what I experienced with the descriptions of different authors. One experience impressed me deeply and marked a turning point. I enjoyed looking at a certain book in which I found exact drawings of different trees. Then I noticed that the drawing of a tree brought about the same experiences in me as the actual tree. This experience I could repeat with different drawings. Through the drawing I was in a position to experience the being of a tree. I did not need to look for the tree in nature; a drawing was sufficient. This was an overwhelming experience; it was my first provable spiritual experience. It was not the sense perception that had allowed me to perceive the being of a tree, but an image, a drawing of this particular tree. Through it I had come into connection with the being of the tree. This experience was repeated numerous times and was always confirmed.

In time my perception awakened for the substantial essence in nature. I began to meet beings in the elemental world. For me those were always surprising meetings. I experienced that I could trust certain beings. I asked them about their tasks, but also inquired what their needs and wishes were, and I tried to fulfil those. Often I was called to certain places. Thus, I was led to places where elementals usually assemble. I learned more and more about their world. I was always met with extraordinary politeness and with trust, which moved me deeply. Many of their secrets were revealed to me and much of what I learned seemed, at first, quite unbelievable. Occasionally I did not trust my eyes and ears. When I asked questions about what I saw and heard, the attending elemental beings were amused, but also estranged, and looked at me in a mocking way. Or they laughed at me and shook their heads, unable to understand how far removed human beings were from the spiritual reality of the earth. They found it especially unbelievable—scandalous—that they experienced this with *me*, someone who had been granted access into their realm.

There was nothing left for me to do, other than to get used to dealing with beings from the elemental world. I often received visitors, read to them or simply listened to them, writing down what they wanted to communicate to me. This resulted in a large number of texts. Furthermore, many of the beings enjoyed being sketched.

I also realized that those meetings were always connected to certain tasks for me. The elementals had questions and requests of me, which they shared. One can well imagine that it was not always easy to fulfil these wishes. I did, however, try to do what I could.

Mostly the questions were concerned with caring for and healing the earth, which is in the interest of the elemental beings. Of course, I met many beings who were in an abominable state; from them I heard the loudest calls. It took some time until I became able to develop a certain confidence in caring for elemental beings and their locations. This work has become my most favorite activity, right up to this day. With my family, with friends, and also alone, I make short and long journeys for the care of beings of the elemental world in various landscapes.

These trips allow me to have experiences that are extremely valuable for me. Every landscape speaks its own language, and every landscape and its beings receive a human being in a different way. It is an exciting task to adapt to ever new and different landscapes. My journeys often lead me into cities. I have been informed again and again about the great significance the elemental beings of the cities have for the development of the humans.

Through actual meetings with various landscapes, I won insights into the deep connection that exists between humans and the earth. I was able to recognize that every landscape has a relationship to a certain aspect of the human being. I recognized the profound connection that exists between the human being and the earth.

School of Life

My experiences with the elemental beings have led me to see them as beings who do not stand in a neutral relationship to humans, but who wish to teach and inform us. The higher elemental beings, especially, convey this wish to me.

This observation rests on the fact that these more highly evolved elementals feel attracted to human beings. They wish to support them. The human being is a being for whom their attention is meant; they want to be heard and seen by us. They look for opportunities to communicate with us. In the information they share with humans, generally more is living than the specific needs expressed by the individual elemental being that reveals itself.

Often it can be observed that when an individual elemental being speaks to a human being, much more is expressed than what comes from it alone. Through this single elemental being, a whole, great world is communicated. Often it happens that one elemental speaks to a human being as if out of an entire chorus of differentiated spirit beings. This chorus can be made up of beings that far surpass the one elemental speaking. Often there is a higher intention behind what is expressed by a single elemental. It is not only the need of this elemental that wants to be heard, but this single being becomes a member in an even larger meaningful context through its communication to the human.

In the course of the last years I have learned ever more to observe what the beings of the elemental world want to tell me. I have often asked them when I had questions, and attempted to follow their advice. I have also occasionally brought them the questions of other human beings. In most cases, when one brings questions to the world of the elementals, these are joyous, even humorous gatherings. Out of a wish for truthfulness that lives in them, they gladly place themselves into the service of human beings who approach them for sure advice. But there are also many beings in which the wish to help is united with a roguish mischief that is impossible to imitate. Sometimes they really make fun of one. However, they do not do this in order to mock, but rather to emphasize that their advice is important. Especially when they make fun of me I notice that there is a deep relationship between us. Yet there are also very serious spirits among the elemental beings. Mischief and humor are only one side of their nature; they can also address a human being in a very serious way. I was very impressed by an experience I had a year ago in the spring. I stood before a young tree, which I observed intensively; it was blossoming, and a number of bees flew from one blossom to the next. It was a Cornelian cherry. The sight of this tree touched me, although I did not know why. After a while I suddenly heard the words, "When does what is broken come together again? For how long will it still continue?" I was overwhelmed by the pain that lay in these words. I felt that this young tree experienced existentially the state of the life conditions of the earth. I remained a few more minutes before the tree, knowing well that it was not a matter of giving an answer. It was sufficient to have heard the question and to further occupy my thoughts with it.

I had and still have interactions with many elemental beings that possess the extraordinary ability to answer everyday questions. They even like answering questions—that surprised me at the beginning. Through their path of development they are prepared to stand, helpfully, by the side of the human being. This may explain why I chose for this book the title, *School of the Elemental Beings*. Beings of the elemental world have become my teachers. This school exists; and individual human beings, and also human communities, live in it. This school exists even if it cannot be directly perceived; and this school is also effective even when one does not know anything about it. Every human being is part of this school because it is nothing other than a part of our destiny. The beings of the elemental world have an important task. Destiny works through them; as spiritual beings, they are integral in the effectiveness of human karma. One can even say that in this task lies their highest and most earnest mission. When they are active in this way, they stand in the service of the highest spiritual beings of the cosmos.

The more one awakens to the beings of the elemental world, the more one can accept an inner relationship to the lessons that they teach humanity. It is the wish and hope connected with this book to make a contribution for humans to awaken to these beings that build a part of our school of life.

New Abilities of Perception

More and more people are having experiences through which they attain certainty that the earth has a spiritual life. They receive impressions of a world behind the sense world. These impressions are often very delicate and inconspicuous. Particularly among young people one astoundingly often finds the remarkable ability to perceive spiritually. It can seem as though they have natural access to the spiritual levels of perception. It shows that in the last decades a fundamental change has taken place in the relationship of the human being to the earth and its spiritual life. It has become easier to "read" in the spirit. Souls are much less separated from what one can call the spiritual earth.

One can observe that the veil between the spiritual and the physical worlds has become thinner. The suprasensory world opens up ever wider for the seeking human being. This means that the spiritual dimensions of the earth will gradually be recognized again. The earth awakens from a sleep that covered it like a blanket, which in earlier times only a few special people were granted to penetrate. What was once an initiation into the mysteries of the spiritual life will become a reality of daily life for more and more people. Spiritual secrets of life will no longer be kept hidden behind closed temple gates. Increasingly, they will become the possession of all people.

These observations are important not only for humans, but also for the elemental beings. They are beings deeply connected with the earth and its development. For this reason, the fact that the boundaries of the physical and spiritual worlds are becoming more permeable releases very intense reactions among the elementals. I could observe elemental beings that looked at young human beings who have a natural gift of clairvoyance and were shaken by a shudder of amazement. They were unable to recover because they were so completely overwhelmed with astonishment. Today there are children through whom the elementals can literally be distracted from their tasks. There are young people who merely through their appearance on earth can cause a transformation, a change in the elemental world. Among the elemental beings the emergence of these human beings is an important event. Today it is important to know about these things. Especially in a time when the human being faces great problems, one should be conscious of changes that occur in the human's innermost being. The elemental beings gather great hope from the observations they make when they look at young people, and also confidence, which enables them to master their tasks even in difficult times.

Pointing out these changes in humanity is in accordance with the wishes of the elementals. Because they are spiritual beings that do not enter our sense world, they are very sensitive to spiritual changes. They have strong and influential experiences through the humans they meet. What kind of people are in their environment, and what they do, feel, and think, is extremely important for the elementals. They observe us—our doings and our development—with great attention.

II.
NATURE SPIRITS

Soul movements (Denmark)

The Tree Spirits

The tree spirits are highly evolved beings of the elemental world. On the one hand, they have the task of protecting the tree in which they live; on the other, they accompany the path of humanity. The tree spirits form a group of beings that are connected with the destiny of human beings. But their influence on humans has abated. The tasks that they carried in the past have been placed into the responsibility of human beings. The tree spirits express this in the following words:

> The old mystery and initiation schools were in one way or another always connected with trees. The tree beings were counted as guides of the human beings into the spiritual world. When humans died, they left the world through the trees. The trees are also the oldest mothers of human beings, because in trees they saw guides who led young souls to the earth. For this reason the reverence for trees was a widespread ancient practice of worship. In all cultures the tree spirits were seen as beings that possessed highly evolved spiritual skills. Nothing has really changed. The only thing that has changed is that the tree spirits have had to refrain from teaching humans out of themselves. The old mystery places, in which a person was introduced by the teachers into the secrets of the trees, and also of the plants, the stars, and the earth, are in ruins. It had to happen. Human beings have changed. They recognize more and more that they carry a great responsibility for themselves.

The pupils of the old Mystery Centers did not have these responsibilities. It was decided for them. They were meant to be pupils. Today no outer authority can determine that a human being is a pupil. Only the individual can say that of himself or herself.

In spite of this, the spirits of the trees have kept the task of supporting and aiding humans on their path of development. But the spirits have had to learn to be silent. They had to hold back, because humans have to experience what it means to follow this path alone, out of themselves. They had to become acquainted with solitude. Today all human beings know what it means to be alone. They know the silence that is created when they themselves become silent. This is an important experience. It is important to experience the pain when the cosmos ceases to speak; when the earth becomes silent; when the earth looks as if it were dead. This experience of a silent, quiet earth had to be experienced by humanity. For this reason the beings of the elemental world, including the tree spirits, had to hold back. This is more difficult than you would think. Because you have forgotten how to listen, and because you no longer take the earth seriously, you have made many blunders and mistakes.

But now conditions are such that we may quietly, softly begin to speak again. We are allowed to come again to the fore and turn to attentive, listening souls. Fortunately, there are more and more people who can listen and are devoted to listening. We are allowed to speak again. Whoever can hear us will be able to notice what happiness and relief it brings us.

What do we say to the listening human souls? We say: Do not give up. Let nobody take away your conviction; look at the doubts but do not allow them to win the upper hand. For you are meant to know that the physical and the spiritual earth have again come closer together. What was separated for so long will slowly, slowly come together again. The worlds press into one another again. Let this news give you hope. You can walk more freely and upright because you know that you are not alone in the universe, but protected and guided by the spiritual world. The angels have not given up being there for you. Do not believe those who try to tell you there is a "nothing." There cannot be "nothing," because where the physical world ends, another world begins. This is the spiritual world. These two worlds reach directly into each other. From a certain point of view these two very different worlds are one. However, you stand at the threshold of both worlds. Learn to know the honor that it signifies to be allowed to stand at the threshold, because it is a special distinction. You will have experiences at this threshold that no other being can have. Your experiences will result in a great accumulation of knowledge for the high and highest beings of the spiritual world. Therefore, everyone who lives at this threshold, thus human beings, will be rewarded in manifold ways. This reward is freedom.

The spirits of the trees stand by your side when you stand at the threshold. They are your brothers that have been sent to you by the spiritual world to hold, sustain and support you, so that you remain standing and do not fall over. For to fall is, of course, not difficult; it happens relatively quickly and easily. We are there to hold you. Take this information seriously because it can lead you to discover further the meaning of the role we play in your life.

The tree spirit is bound to the physicality of the tree. It leaves the tree only when it dies. It enters the tree when the tree begins to develop its own individual shape. Tree seedlings do not yet have a tree spirit, and saplings a few years old have as yet no tree spirit living in them. Only in time will a tree spirit enter. The moving into a tree is a great event in the elemental world. One can compare it with a wedding: a spirit being weds a living tree. A decision stands behind this wedding, because the spirit being unites itself completely with the living tree. The spirit surrenders to the earthly world. This is a major event for a tree spirit that is a high-standing elemental being.

Only through the entrance of the tree spirit does the sapling become a tree. Through this it is raised to a special being in the plant world. The young tree will at this moment be placed into the life and developmental stream to which only trees belong. The being and the task of trees can really be understood only when one makes an imagination of this life stream.

In order to understand the importance of the tree spirit for the tree, it is necessary to look at the sphere from which this being comes. One-year-old herbs can manage to live without such a being. Only wood-forming plants that are several years old have a special spirit being living in them. It originates from the earth, and rises into the trees. It is more accurate to say that it originates from the realm of the metals. The tree spirits were once spirits of metals. Before they move into a tree and begin to live in it, they have undergone a development as spirits of metals. In that phase they were strongly given over to the earth and its cosmic processes. The effect of the cosmic beings lives in the metals. The cosmos sounds forth in the metals. Through the beings of the metals the earth receives cosmic gifts; metals are messengers of the planetary spheres. The tree spirits bring with them the wisdom of the cosmos, which they absorbed as beings of metals. Only through that wisdom do trees become what they are for human beings. They become teachers of human beings. It is not an exaggeration to say that when we go to the trees and occupy ourselves with them, we enter a university that teaches us what the earth and the human being receive from the cosmos.

The tree spirits bear knowledge about the great mysteries and secrets of the earth. Through them one can become conscious of the cosmic life foundations of the earth. That is the reason tree spirits have always functioned as teachers of humanity, and why they had tasks in the Mystery culture of humanity.

Tree spirits are beings that are deeply connected to the seasons of the year. Through the course of the year, the tree spirit does not always live in the same relationship to the tree. In the winter it has a very different relationship to its tree than during the summer or at other times of the year. In the summer it is lifted out of the tree. The tree spirit is present in the tree, but its being also stretches far out into the area that encompasses the tree from the outside. In the winter, however, the tree spirit will go back into the earth where it originated. It lets go of the tree to such an extent that it is connected only with the roots. It then lies in the earth, and penetrates ever further into the earth during the cold time of the year. When it becomes warmer it rises up again from below, and it extends again into the tree.

The life that it lives in the summer is different from the life it leads in the winter. During different seasons it is connected with very different situations of reality. One could say that in the summer the tree spirit lives exhaled in the wisdom of the light of the earth; and in the winter, on the other hand, it lives surrendered to the wisdom of the warmth of the earth. In the summer the buds for the new year are formed out of the forces of the light. In the winter the spirit of the tree unites with the sacred forces of the earth, with the realm from which it originated. During the winter it experiences its own renewal; while in the summer it is the tree that experiences its renewal through the buds.

In the spring the spirit is most strongly bound to the tree. Its whole consciousness is dedicated to the unfolding of the leaves and the young shoots, as well as the entire process of tree growth. It is at that time that it is absolutely the spirit of the tree. In the autumn it begins to withdraw. It lets the tree be, and separates from the close union with it. In the spring, the tree serves most fully as the dwelling of the tree spirit. In the fall, the spirit separates from this connection. It is necessary for the tree spirit to separate. It cannot remain any longer but needs to renew itself by uniting with the wintery earth.

For the tree spirit, autumn is the time when it remembers what it has experienced during the summer. In the spring it lives from the forces that it was able to gather during the winter on its way through the earth, and passes on to the tree what it has gathered. While the tree spirit lives in the summer with its consciousness in what happens around the earth, it has only a dull experience of itself. In the fall, when it begins to withdraw, pictures arise like memories of what it has experienced during the condition of the earth's time of exhalation in the summer. These are true pictures that arise within. In these images it sees the great connections of the life of the earth. During the summer it knows nothing of what it experiences. But it takes the memories along on the way into the wintery earth. With these true images that arise within like memories, the tree spirit teaches the elemental beings that live in the tree or near it. Therefore, many elementals look to the trees in the fall, because they wish to catch a glimpse of something from these truth-filled pictures that arise in the memory of the tree spirits. Through these memory pictures, the elementals of the tree, the spirits of the leaves, the beings of the roots, and those of the bark, become dazed. They observe an event to which they themselves have no access. The connection with the more highly evolved tree spirit allows them the possibility to enter deeply into the memory pictures and downright revel in them. This indulging means that they say farewell to the physical conditions of the earth. Life fades away; it withdraws. The leaves wilt and the sap becomes more sluggish. The elementals that are now freed because the life of the tree is dwindling, dissolve into summer dreams. They become reconciled with the larger cosmic life, while they leave the life that connects them with the tree. They lose themselves in the tree spirit's summer memories.

In the winter the tree spirit sinks into the earth. It unites not with the physical earth, but with the spiritual earth. Its own being becomes imbued with the spiritual earth and partakes in its secrets. The original spiritual earth becomes alive in it. The tree spirit descends with its being down to the original condition of the earth and experiences the earth's spiritual development while wandering through it. By doing this it obtains the life forces that it needs as a tree spirit.

The tree spirits of various kinds of trees differ in their nature. In the tree spirit the respective kind of tree is expressed. The tree spirit of a birch, for example, is different from the spirit of a walnut tree. Every tree spirit points with its being to the kind of tree it lives in.

Therefore, an accurate study of a tree as it shows itself to the senses of the human being is a path to finding access to the tree spirit. The tree spirit experiences our loving gazing at the tree as a blessing. When one wants to do something good for a tree, one needs to do no more, at first, than to view it with devotion. For a tree spirit it is a great experience when the tree—that is its abode, its body—is attentively looked at by a human being. It experiences a loving, conscious gaze as a kind of stroking. The tree spirit does not experience the outer shape of the tree or form of a tree as separate from itself. By looking at the tree, one touches the tree spirit. Through this it awakens to the world of human beings. For a tree spirit, being looked at is indeed an awakening experience through which it meets a specific person.

Every tree species is an expression of an independent sphere of life. Through the study of the different kinds of trees one gains access to these life spheres. They point to meaningful spiritual archetypes. Only sensitive and patient research leads to the ability to grasp the archetypes of particular tree species. The tree spirit is the spirit being that provides a connection between the searching human and the archetypes of the tree species. Through the tree spirit, this archetype speaks to the searching human being. The tree spirit is the being that one can approach when one is interested in getting to know the archetype of the tree.

A sensitive study of sense phenomena leads to the cognition of the archetypes of particular species of trees. One can also conceive of the spiritual beings as a unity, as a group of spiritual beings. I have received many messages from different tree spirits that point to a unity of tree spirits. One may speak of a circle of trees. Here are the words of a tree spirit about this.

> You, dear human beings, trees have created a circle around you. You stand in the center among the tree spirits; and you stand there as representatives of humanity. You cannot hide from the spirits of the

trees, and you do not need to. Their presence might make you wonder, or even frighten you. This does not have to be so, because they are there to your advantage. This circle was drawn around you so that you do not forget to grow; the trees show you how one grows. And they also show you how part of growing is letting go; how death belongs to growing. The trees die, but they die easily. You pass through a gate with every tree that stands before you, a gate of life! Feel how properly you are accepted by this gate. Feel embraced by the tree when you step toward it. Experience how every tree is a different gate through which you enter. You experience the circle of trees most easily when you see gates in the trees, which are there for you. For the circle of trees consists of the most varied gates, but every gate is incomplete without the others. That is why the trees surround you and take you into their midst.

These are thoughts that can help us to live deeply into the nature of the tree spirits. The tree spirits live for the trees in which they reside, but they live also for human beings. They want to serve humans, but they want to do this in a very specific way. They want to do it in such a way that they challenge us to take the first steps by ourselves. It is the secret of our time that the spiritual beings of the earth wait for the human being. They do not speak when we do not lend them our ear and our inner sense. They depend on the awakening of this inner sense in the human being. The conditions have reversed, in that the spiritual world withdraws and leaves the task to humanity to develop the freedom of our being. The variety of trees—the circle that they have created around humanity—has especially to do with the development of freedom. They form a circle so that the human being in their midst can come to know his or her freedom and develop it. They step back, but they do not withhold from us the forces they can give and want to offer. However, we are challenged to decide in freedom to come to know the circle of the trees and their gifts.

Wood is the fundamental substance of the trees. Indeed, many secrets are connected to wood; it is a special and unique substance. It belongs to the wondrous substances of the world.

> Wood is our secret. If you want to penetrate our secret, you have to understand the nature of wood. It is a sacred substance. Only through it does the possibility exist for us to be present on the earth in the trees. In the wood is He, the Christ. He chose wood, chose to live in it. In wood He transcends all time. He has chosen to die on wood, and to live on in wood. Therefore, he can be seen in it. In the different kinds of wood live the different aspects of the being of Christ. You can ask every kind of wood about the characteristic of Christ's being that it harbors. Together the different kinds of wood provide a living picture of His comprehensive being. You approach Him when you study the wood, and when you study the trees. Because the Christ has made peace with the trees, we are His children. At anytime He can speak through any one of us. He can reveal Himself in each one of us at any time. Our importance and the tree's importance for you lie in the fact that we are His children. He is our Father because He has shed His blood over us; we are sanctified through His blood. The wood is holy because He died on it.

The wood was the substance that stood earliest in the power of the resurrection. The trees and their spirits were able to spread the Christ message immediately. They knew before any other being on earth knew that He had risen and that the earth is redeemed. Yes, it is redeemed. For He is in the wood. Our attraction to the wood, our repeated dwelling in the trees is connected with the reality that we experience Him there; that we know Him in us there; and that we can serve Him there as nowhere else in the world.

Elemental beings change and develop, and this development is subject to certain cycles. Because there are so many kinds of elemental beings, it is not easy to work out general laws of this development. And yet one can say that the beings of the elemental world are continually growing in their development. They develop further by completing certain steps of transformation and taking on more encompassing and complex tasks. One can say that they learn. The higher development of an elemental being consists in the fact that what was learned through one task is available for the next task, in a certain sense.

Now we will describe how tree spirits are prepared to fulfill their tasks as guardians of a tree. In the elemental world a tree spirit is an important and therefore high-ranking being. This shows in its developmental process. It was already mentioned that tree spirits, before they connect themselves with a tree, are beings that live in the earth. There they live beside other beings that represent the planetary forces in the earth. In the organism of the earth spiritual spheres exist, which are completely influenced by streams of forces of individual planets. There the beings live that later rise to be tree spirits. In these places in the earth they undergo a very essential schooling. Through it they become able to develop out of themselves the strength to hold together the spiritual form of a tree. Their tasks consist of creating the spiritual framework for a tree. This is a demanding task. Within the earth they are prepared for this task.

Before the developing tree spirits undertake the preparation for this step in the earth at the side of the planetary beings, they have already made a still earlier step in their development. This consisted of having lived as cosmic beings in the spiritual circumference of the earth. There they lived as beings in the spiritual "vestments" or spirit bodies of angels. They left these cosmic spheres step by step as they descended down to earth to complete their schooling in the earth. On this path they take on increasingly more spiritual earthly substance.

The significance of tree spirits lies in the fact that after they have descended out of the cosmos, they penetrate the earth; and then they appear for the first time in the physical world in the trees. They are on a path that empowers them to be elemental beings that are the bearers of high cosmic forces. Actually, through the spirits of trees, a life stream flows that is essential for the earth and the human being. One perceives a spiritual chalice when one directs one's attention to this life stream that penetrates the earth through the path of development of a tree spirit. This chalice is connected with the special substance that is wood. It is offered by the spirits of the trees to human beings who are searching for the truth of existence. When we search for the truth, when we have the wish to fathom the mysteries of existence, we can place trust in the fact that the tree spirits will unite with this wish. If we bring peace and patience with us, we can consult the trees about even the weightiest matters. We can receive answers to our questions from the trees.

Verse of Blessing from a Tree Spirit to Human Beings

Go
Out of the strength of your own being
Let nothing divert you
From your path

One has only one's own path
One's life's footprints
Leading
Guiding
One over the Earth

And they lay themselves over the Earth
Like a golden pattern
That calls you
When you return

Tree Fairies

The trees are extremely important for the beings of the elemental world. Elemental meetings take place under the vaulted and peaceful roof of the trees, during which they receive instructions from higher beings. Trees also stand between the other world and this one. This is connected with the substance of wood. The living wood is the substantial foundation for the other world and this world meeting in the trees. The fact that trees stand at this threshold of worlds is also the reason that very specific elemental beings are born in the trees. We will now get to know some of these elementals.

Very specific beings are born through each kind of tree. The beings that originate in the Linden tree are of a different nature than those that are born from an Ash tree or a Larch. As a general rule, only a mature tree can give birth to elemental beings. Tree spirits of young and old trees are far too occupied with the tree itself to dedicate themselves to the birth of elemental beings. But this applies only in general. There are also very old trees that do not lose this gift. It is even normal that Larch trees remain birthplaces for elemental beings far into old age.

The beings that are born through the trees belong to the group known as the fairies. They are spirits that stand between the elements of air and light. Fairies are beings that are deeply connected with human beings. They also appear in many fairy tales as beings that mediate between humans and higher realms of the earth. Fairies are messengers that move back and forth between humans and the beings of the higher hierarchies. They are spirits of destiny that take on guardianship of individuals, but also groups of people. It is absolutely possible that for a time a family has a fairy as its guardian spirit. But one can also find fairies that protect and try to guide individual people. Small children are always protected by a fairy. They are children's playmates and protective spirits, which are sent to them from the spiritual world.

Every tree species brings forth fairies with specific tasks. Out of the Elder tree, fairies arise that have the special task to protect children. Protective spirits come forth from the Elder that take on the task of guarding children during their sleep, as well as when they play.

The Linden tree gives birth to fairies that dedicate themselves to the social life of people. Their task is predominantly to clear away obstacles that create problems in mutual understanding. They achieve that by standing between people, or among people in community, to "clear the air." In this way misunderstandings can be avoided or cleared up.

The spirit of the Hazelnut tree brings forth fairies that help individual people. They help people to find their own individual path. They provide soul forces to reach clarity about our own tasks and motives in life. These fairies go before the people they have chosen. When we are in a soul mood that allows the fairy to reach us, it can appear to us. This can take place when we let go of our rigidly structured thoughts. When we begin to dream a little, the fairy can then send us certain thoughts or images, which can become a pointer for the direction in which we should go.

The fairies that come to birth in the Larch are beings with a special power. These too serve the individual. They place gifts at our disposal through which we can connect ourselves with heaven and earth. In this way they serve the inner balance of human beings, which is a prerequisite for unfolding our own individual being.

The fairy of the Hornbeam tree wants to acquaint human beings with deep secrets of the earth and of life. It wishes to lead us into the depths of soul, as well as into the depths of the earth. This is a fairy of truthfulness that wishes to speak to the human through the Hornbeam.

The fairies of the Hawthorn and of the Olive tree are active in a similar direction. They also are interested in sharing the mysteries of the earth and of our development. The Hawthorn fairy speaks more to the masculine side of the human being, while the fairy of the Olive tree speaks more to the feminine side.

The fairy of the Ash, this holy tree, speaks of the mysteries that have been guarded, protected, and passed on by people since ancient times. These mysteries have to be taken up, newly grasped, and passed on by each generation. These insights that humanity has attained can become fruitful only when every generation dedicates itself to these treasures of wisdom, takes them up anew, and develops them further according to their times. Wisdom is a growing treasure that turns into its opposite, however, when one leaves it as it is. What is known can grow further only when it is renewed and transformed. Thus, a strong force of renewal and transformation comes from the fairy of the Ash tree.

"Fairy hole" or "hiding place" is what the fairies call the gate through which they appear when they are born in the trees. For them it is the gate leading from the world where they normally live into the world of human beings. They truly wish that humans would come to understand the significance of the trees as birthplaces for elemental beings. They know that it is not very difficult for humans to gain access to the other world through the trees. We need only to want to get to know the spiritual dimension that is present for us on earth through the beings of the trees. This dimension is not far away; it is close to the life of people. It is only that humans know far too little about the collaborative work that is constantly being offered out of great loyalty by the trees. But we who take up this interest and begin to dedicate ourselves to the trees out of the forces of our consciousness will in time recognize the gifts of the trees and their co-dwellers, the fairies.

The Fairy of the Rose and the Fairy of the Oak

Whoever studies in detail the world of the plants will have the experience that the Rose takes a special place among them. The fairy being of the Rose (more precisely, the Dog Rose) has a special closeness with human beings. It wishes to be heard by people. Thus, it speaks:

> I will never grow old. The child that I am, I am for eternity. The one who searches for me will find the child. That, however, is the soul child that every one of you carries and knows, that in me and through me looks into the earthly world. I lose everything that I am given; I cannot keep anything. That is me. Therefore one cannot demand anything from me, because I give away everything that I have anyway. Whoever meets me meets giving. I give without keeping anything, without looking after myself. That is, however, the force out of which I grow. Giving is really a growing force, a force that leads to more.

Giving is an important soul force. But it needs a sheath of protection. The Rose fairy does not possess this encompassing faculty. It is completely filled with the force of the child who surrenders to everything. But it is the Rose itself that provides the protection that the child needs. Indeed, the Rose fairy, a delicate and easily injured being, seeks its protection in the Rose. The strong life forces of the Rose, its resilience and endurance, offer to the vulnerable fairy what it needs in order to live under earthly conditions. The Rose as a strong plant is a secure home in which the fairy can live.

The Oak has a similar task in relation to its fairy. This fairy also is a delicate being. It is not childlike, but is nevertheless vulnerable. It is the guardian of certain feminine forces. It mediates the soul characteristic connected with the conceiving of new spiritual life: the force of Intuition. The Oak fairy protects the force necessary for surrendering to what wants to speak from the spiritual world to the human being. The Oak tree is the perfect abode for it; it does not need to let go of its delicacy and openness, and yet it still has a home. The Oak fairy wants to pass on this gift of Intuition to the human beings who approach it. It can do this all the more easily when we understand the truth that going to a tree is always a meeting with beings that must remain invisible and yet wish to work together and cooperate with human beings.

The Spirit of the Forest

Elemental beings are subject to certain developmental laws, and they fulfill their respective tasks only for a certain length of time. When the time has come, they lay their work aside and undergo a transformation that places them into a position to take on another task. The transformation that an elemental being experiences between two tasks may be quite far reaching. Through suprasensory observation one can follow the developmental paths of various elemental beings. Now that we have shown the path of development of the tree spirits, we will describe the path of transformation of another elemental being.

One very interesting being of the elemental world is the spirit of the forest. It is the elemental being one can also call the guardian of the forest. It is a highly evolved being that likes to hide from humans. When it shows itself, it seems a little sullen and taciturn; it does not like to use too many words. But whatever it says carries weight. One can hear from it quite poignant facts about oneself, and if one is not prepared it could be quite frightening. It is generally a being that quickly gains respect through its ways. Its task is to create a living center for the elemental beings of the forest. It is something like their father; the elemental beings look to it with great reverence, and the tree spirits also are very fond of it.

When one meets the spirit of a forest, one experiences a being that looks surprisingly wild. It is covered over with earth and bark. Its hair is matted and reaches nearly to the ground. Its walk is heavy. When it wants to reveal secrets to a human being, it offers an open hand. This hand is huge and soft and from it streams peace. One would love to lie down and cuddle up as if it were a cradle. In its hand it holds certain symbols, forms, or pictures, which it shows to the human. These symbols hold in encrypted form what it would like to tell the human, but they are not always easy to interpret. The spirit of the forest wants one to be astonished about what it shows, and to begin to decode the symbols for oneself. It says:

> Full of mysteries is the earth; full of mysteries is life. Never will the secrets be revealed to the first naive look. For that more is required. You must exert yourself to solve the riddle that I give you. Otherwise, you will not be able to use the gift you receive through me.

This spirit fulfilled a different task before it appeared as spirit of the forest. It was a spirit of subterranean water. Such a being is responsible for guarding the water that flows under the surface of the earth. This water is of great significance for the earth and all life on it. It is very important that this subterranean water remain pure, because out of it many elementals arise. For the elemental world, it has a task similar to the amniotic fluid for the developing human: It nourishes the elementals in the first stages of their development. The guardian of the subterranean water lives totally within the damp, watery darkness of the earth. In spite of this, one cannot notice any heaviness in it. Rather, it is a light-filled and very agile being. It is very difficult to perceive this being; it never rises to the light of day. It would not be able to endure the direct sunlight shining onto the light whose bearer it is itself. It needs the darkness of the earth emphatically.

The forest spirit arises out of the guardian of the subterranean water. One can still notice what it has been before; it clearly shows the signs of having been a water being. Even the shyness toward light that is characteristic of the guardian of the water can still be found in the spirit of the forest. It too is deeply bound to the processes of substances, as is apparent from the fact that it has chosen the earthy ground as its clothes.

Suprasensory observation reveals that the guardian beings of the subterranean waters themselves arise out of beings who live in the light. These beings of light live in the light above the earth's surface. One can also describe this realm as the aura of a landscape. It is filled with various beings of light that are of very different quality. The beings that transform into the aforementioned water beings have an ordering function in the light aura of the earth. One can say that these beings collect the other, lower light beings, the sylphs, in their own light aura. The more highly developed beings of light appear to be close to the world of angels and provide a transition between the elemental world and the astral world. These are the ones that develop into guardians of subterranean waters; and later, out of these, the spirit of the forest develops.

This example shows how an elemental being goes through different stages of development. Before it can arise as a forest spirit, it has acquired experiences with the element of water, and also with the light-air element. Only then is it given the task to be guardian of the forest. It can be observed that through this sequence of development this being gradually comes closer to the earth and its conditions. At the same time it also slowly approaches the realm of humans. Even as a forest spirit it retains a visible shyness about meeting humans, although at each stage it has gained essential experiences through which it has been prepared for meeting them.

Guardian of the Rocks

A large number of spiritual beings live in the mountains. To describe the life of these mountain elementals would require its own separate presentation. It can be observed that every rock protruding from the masses of rock provides a home for such a guardian being. These spirits of the rocks are silent beings; their work consists of keeping watch. They are elementals that bring a certain quality of consciousness to the place where they live. Through this they produce a force that resists the weight of the mass of stone in a mountain range. It is their task to create a consciousness that serves to hold together the colossal mass of rock and stone. Mountain ranges do not exist of themselves. It is an illusion to believe that anything on the earth exists out of itself. Wherever something holds together, forces and beings are at work through which such a cohesion takes place. This applies also to the mountains, and this is the task of the guardians of the rocks. They are quiet and still spirits, and yet they are wide awake.

In contrast to the gnomes who are born from the depths of the earth, the guardians of the rocks emerge from air beings; they develop from beings of light-imbued air. If one observes the path of development of the guardians of the rocks further back into the past, one can see that originally they arose from warmth. The path of evolution of the guardians of the rocks to the earth proceeds in such a way that they slowly descend through the elements to the earth; they gradually get closer to the earth. As guardians of the rocks they are beings that do not have the same rank as the gnomes; they remain beings of the light. Only because they do not devote themselves to the earth are they able to unfold the strength of consciousness that is needed to fulfill their task. In them the forces of air, light, and warmth are especially alive. Through these alone they can provide a counterforce to the weight of stone and rock. The mountains owe their cohesion to the guardians of the rocks; to their sense for lightness of weight, and their relationship to the elements of light and warmth. The guardians of the rocks are important spirits but very reserved. They do not want to be disturbed; if that happened, the weight that they have been entrusted with would fall away from them.

III.
GATES TO THE ELEMENTAL BEINGS

Birth of Life

How Can One Meet Elemental Beings?

One cannot really tell when and where the path begins that finally leads to a meeting with the elemental beings. It will, in any case, be a winding path, a path of tests and trials. The trials will vary and are different for every human being. It is comforting and, in the end, beneficial to look at the resistances one meets in one's own life as trials of this kind.

Sequences of images in fairy tales are illustrations of the law that resistances are trials that serve development. Indeed, one can read every biography as a fairy tale. In our own lives, all of us come to places where we stand like a hero in a fairy tale. Elemental beings look at human beings in this special way of the fairy tale. Fairy tales give a successful account of how elementals view the life of human beings. For this reason one does a favor to elemental beings when one learns to think in concepts taken from fairy tales. It is thus absolutely a possibility to prepare oneself and adapt for a meeting with the elemental world by awakening to and occupying oneself inwardly with the images that originate in fairy tales. In the fairy tale images there are many examples that point to the life of the elementals. The connection that exists between the life of humans and that of elementals is described in veiled form in fairy tales.

It is possible for human beings to listen to the life-wisdom of nature when they meet it, in order to fathom its wisdom and its mysteries. For this one needs nothing more than time, and often it is indeed only a question of time. Many of the elemental beings cannot understand our complaint that we "don't have time." They are of the opinion that humans who do not even manage their own time give themselves up for lost. We give ourselves up as lost when we lose our influence over time, but the time we have is a very valuable possession. It is precisely the key for coming closer to the beings of the elemental world.

Time develops its fullness only when we forget about it. When one wants to meet the elemental beings, when one goes to a certain place in the countryside, one should make the decision to leave thoughts about time behind. It is much easier to meet the elemental beings when one attempts to place oneself outside the time structure to which one normally belongs. The elemental beings perceive how far an individual human being is bound to a certain time structure and whether the soul subordinates itself to certain influences that are part of the present human culture. They experience as a disturbing influence our being bound to specific concepts having to do with time. They cannot endure it when we subordinate ourselves to a time structure that we did not create ourselves. For this reason it is important to consciously shield ourselves from such ideas connected with time. In other words, it is important that one becomes free from the idea that one has only a certain set amount of time available. The more we are able to enter into a mood of timelessness, the more easily the beings of the elemental world can perceive us. I myself hand over my management of time to the elemental beings. I ask them, for example, to show me when I must leave again so that I will not arrive too late for my next appointment. In most cases, this has worked well.

In the beginning it is necessary to take this step into the mood of timelessness consciously. One can designate a certain place on the way (a special tree, a bridge, or the edge of the forest) as the transition into timelessness, into the land of dreams or fairy tales. It feels as if one goes through a gate. In time one will notice that such gates really do exist. There are fairy tale gates in a landscape, through which one can enter in order to leave behind all that could be disturbing, so that elementals can look clearly at the human being. Human beings definitely cannot, out of themselves, force access to a meeting with the elementals. These meetings are granted to us by the beings of the elemental world; we are received by the elementals. We can approach them only if they allow us to do so. Whoever wants to discover the world of the elementals is dependent on permission to enter their realm. There is no other way to come to them; otherwise, they would simply leave us alone. They show themselves to someone only when that person is deemed worthy of it. It is precisely for this reason that one has to undergo trials to reach this required worthiness. Our relationship with time, our handling of time, is an important criterion for this.

For the elemental beings, free time brought to them by a human being is really a gift. For them, time is space. The time offered gives them the opportunity to appear to a human being. They feel attracted to this space that arises around the human being; yes, even accepted. Something enters their world that they cannot generate. A spiritual space is formed because human beings make a decision out of their own volition. We decide to get involved in laws and particular characteristics that perhaps appear unusual and strange to us. This is because when the soul develops timelessness—one can also say a lack of desires or wishes—then it lets go of the idiosyncrasies of the human cultural world. The thread that binds the soul to business and to the demands of the human world becomes thinner and thinner. When this thread tears, when the soul leaves behind what has tied it to the world of human culture, then it has separated itself from what estranges it from the elemental world. Only now does the soul become visible in its beauty and radiance to the beings of the elemental world. There falls away from it the veils that the elementals cannot penetrate when they look at the human being. It is not up to the elementals to take these veils away.

Only the soul mood of a human being fashions the spiritual space through which the beings of the elemental world can meet the human. This space is the spiritual house in which the human soul and the elementals meet. It is the prerequisite for facilitating development. This is because meetings between elemental beings and humans are always connected to development, which wants to find its fulfillment. These meetings that take place between humans and elementals are always significant and essential for the participants. Perhaps the importance of such an occurrence for the human being will reveal itself only much later, or perhaps there is an immediate grasping of the situation. Either way, we feel deeply touched in soul when we notice that beings of the elemental world turn toward us. It is really true that they come to us more than we to them. We can only prepare ourselves for this; everything else we have to leave to them.

Many elemental beings are curious. Their eyes are full of expectation, and they show great interest toward the one who enters their realm. However, one can also meet elemental beings that are angry toward the human being and hold back, waiting. They actually withdraw when one approaches them, or they even turn away. In the beginning one experiences resentment and aversion, and it takes some time before one has gained their trust.

There are also many elementals that suffer. They appear grey and lifeless, even angry without really being so. They are forced to live and appear in a form that does not correspond with their true being. Through what they bear as beings of the elemental world, what they have taken up through humans, they have become estranged from their own original being.

Often they are immobile; their suprasensory sheath is damaged; or they are depressed and lethargic. It can even happen that a human is chased away because the elementals at a particular location have had so many bad experiences with people that they want to avoid any further contact. In such a case one is showered with curses. Of course, then it is wrong to give in and to walk away, because these beings are not themselves. They suffer because they have taken on too much that is foreign to who they are. One can win their confidence if one simply remains where one is, and waits. They will recognize that one is serious and is not deceived by their display of anger. For they are not themselves angry, they have been made so. The resentment and hatred they radiate is not their own.

Now one can begin to offer help. Setting up burning wax candles, or burning incense or scented resins can be especially effective in such a case. It can also make sense to light a small fire. Then they will come to warm themselves because often they suffer from the coldness of soul that they have taken on. They could also desire that one read to them or sing. Perhaps after a while they really look to being closer to a human, and let themselves be touched, stroked, or massaged. This may sound strange to someone who has not had such experiences. However, there are occasions when the radiance of the human aura can help elementals to reconnect with the origin of their own being.

Speaking with Elemental Beings

The elemental beings wish for humans to come into contact with them. They have a great need to hear us; they would like us to speak to them. We ought to overcome our shyness about conversing with them. The human voice speaking in a loving way to them arouses among them a feeling of great well-being. They draw love and warmth from the meeting with a human, when this meeting happens out of love and devotion. This is something that they miss. In earlier times it was completely natural for humans to have conversations with nature spirits. People talked to beings, to plants, animals, and things in their ordinary dealings. They knew that it can make sense to talk even to objects, because they knew or suspected that spiritual beings live also in those. People felt far less distant in relation to their surroundings. Although it does not make sense simply to bring back this outdated situation, still the need of the elemental spirits for the attention, the words and the voice of humans is unbroken. And even if the people of today do not find it natural to speak with things and beings in nature, it is still possible for them to relearn it. A yearning lives among the elementals for the stream that flows from humans to them. But this is a stream of attention, a stream of speaking.

For the elemental beings, human beings are a book with seven seals. They would like to ask many questions of us. When we stop in a place in nature, then usually we are being observed by some elemental beings. Shyly they approach to see who is there. In most cases they are quite surprised when we notice them. For them it is an unusual and rare experience to be seen by a human being. Each time it is a big event, through which many other elementals are attracted. These beings tell each other that they have met a human who can see or feel them. Generally it does not take them long to show their curiosity by asking a few questions. One is asked what one brings along, or has in one's backpack. When one opens it before their eyes and shows them, it leads to a little folk festival among them. In the shortest time one becomes the center of a whole crowd of beings. They want to know where one got up in the morning, and which path one took to come to them. "Over which place on earth did you direct your footsteps today?" they ask. But they also want to know why one travels alone. For most elementals it is incomprehensible that a human being can be alone. When one is accompanied by others, they wish for the companions to be introduced. They want to know who stands before them; where the people come from, and why they are there. The first questions from the elementals often are, "What are you doing here? Why are you here? What do you want?" Therefore, when one arrives at a location it is never wrong to talk about oneself.

Elemental beings want to be able to take part in experiences one has had in one's life and now carries around. There are always curious ears that are keen to hear whatever we tell them about our path and the experiences that we have had on the way. For this reason they also listen closely when people talk to each other. One can definitely make it a habit to talk about oneself and one's own goals at the places one is passing through. It could become part of a culture to inform elementals of such things.

It is, of course, also possible to read to beings of the elemental world. They like to hear poetry and verses. They especially love fairy tales and the Gospels.

The elemental beings hope that conversations with them become a habit. They would receive great strength through this. Human beings would then be much more easily perceived by them. In fact, humans who begin to speak to them can be much more visible to them. The result is that they can support the work of human beings much better, and can stand by them actively with the great tasks they have to manage.

The Gate of Attentiveness

There is another important gate through which one can reach the beings of the elemental world, the gate of attentiveness. One passes through it by very carefully observing the area of the place where one happens to be. The elementals experience a feeling of well-being when one observes attentively and accurately. They wish one to look attentively and let reverberate in one's own soul what has been seen or experienced with other senses. This echoing in one's own soul nourishes the elementals. They feel what the human being experiences inwardly through what one brings forth with one's existence and work. When one experiences the form of the leaves with one's soul, this brings forth a deep feeling of well-being in elementals of the leaves. They feel recognized and accepted by the human being. One can do the same with twigs and branches of trees, and with all the plants and animals one sees. One can do the same also with the sounds and smells of a place. In the same way, one can awaken the dynamics of a landscape and its topography to new life in one's soul. Everything that a location offers to the senses can reverberate in the soul. One will notice that through this one's relationship with the place changes; one grows together with it. One can do this only because through the intensity of one's own perception one has sent out soul-threads that serve to help the beings of the elemental world come closer to the human and to show themselves.

Reading the Signs of Life

Through the life and existence of the elementals, certain spiritual impulses are incorporated into the physical world. Through these impulses the earth receives its face. Through the entirety of the beings of the elemental world, the earthly reality manifests. We may thank the existence of the elementals that the earth is visible. They are the last stage of a permanently ongoing birthing event through which the physical world comes into appearance. The impulses that are realized through the elemental beings, however, do not come from them. They receive these impulses from beings of higher spiritual worlds. The beings of the elemental world are, therefore, serving spirits. Their service allows spiritual impulses from beings of the higher world to stream to earth and take on form. In this way, through the work of the beings of the elemental world, the plants appear, which we perceive as sense-perceptible forms. The spirits of the plants receive from a higher sphere what comes into being through them and appears as a physical plant. Spiritual plant beings can become active and work in the physical world only through the elementals.

These thoughts help us understand that the elemental beings relate to humans in quite a specific way, because they experience themselves as signs. They experience their existence and their work as a sign language, by means of which they appear before us. When we observe the sense world, we look into what is brought about by the beings of the elemental world. In this world brought about by the elementals, we read when we perceive. Human cognition, therefore, means the reading of signs that appear through the physical world. In the forms, colors, and gestures, in the cycles of life, human beings can read as we would read a script. In observing the things and beings of the world, we see a world of signs. When we perceive, we read the sign language that the beings of the elemental world spread out before us. The elemental beings experience us human beings as "readers" when we perceive.

The first step of cognition is, therefore, to read the signs of the sense world. Through these signs the elemental beings speak to us. The next steps have to do with the deciphering of the sign language. Through this the phenomena of the sense world become clear and understandable. The elemental beings feel themselves to be like single letters of a large book. The language of this book can be learned just as any foreign language can be learned.

"Behold," the elementals call to the human being:

Behold what shows itself to you. Behold with all the senses that you have. And avoid adding anything, but read the signs as they are. It is difficult to read when your soul is not silent. Otherwise, you hear only yourself and interpret the signs according to what you already know. We have slipped into these signs, or we were put into them. It helps us if you learn to read these signs, which we are. It helps us because then we can see that you are prepared to take us into yourself. You accept us when you begin to read what speaks through us."

As we deepen ourselves in this sign language, which is spread out before us through physical reality, we meet the creative activity of the beings of the elemental world. By entering with our feeling into the forms, the colors and processes, we experience these activities in our soul. Now it makes an important difference whether we expect to experience the activity of spiritual beings when we observe the sense world, or if for us a spiritual reality behind the senses does not exist. We would look and observe differently, and the experiences we have would find different paths in our souls. When we take a point of departure from a spiritual reality that speaks through the facts of the material world, then we feel how in every thing or being that we observe, we are faced with a mystery. This mystery wants to reveal itself to us. It is waiting to be seen and understood; the world wants to be recognized and understood.

The elemental beings wish that human beings would read to them. They want to be recognized and known. They do not feel themselves to be beings that want to hide spiritual reality from the human gaze. They reveal the spiritual precisely through what they create. The mysteries of life are revealed through them. Through recognizing and knowing, human beings live into the events of the elemental world. The elemental beings are the revealers of the reality of the spiritual life of the earth. They reveal much more than they hide.

Elemental Beings Look Up to Human Beings

There are many elemental beings that perceive what occurs in the human world. One can definitely feel observed by the beings of the elemental world. When one goes for a walk in nature, one can sometimes be taken hold of by a vague feeling that one is not alone. Although there is no one anywhere near, one feels the presence of a foreign consciousness. Even if one assumes this must be wrong, it is often the case that one is being perceived by beings of the elemental world. For elementals, it is most interesting to observe humans. They like to see what we are doing. The reason for this curiosity is that the beings of the elemental world are deeply connected with the destiny of humans. Their own existence is oriented toward human beings. Their own development is anything but independent from the destiny of human development.

The elemental beings that have a deep connection to the earth element, gnomes and earth spirits, are especially close to humans; in any case, closer than the beings of other elements. But other beings, whose task is to accompany single individuals or groups of humans, also observe humans with great interest and attention. They have experiences through human beings; they experience our perfection, talents, and capabilities. A human's ability to remember, and also to think, creates great astonishment among elementals. They ask again and again how we actually can remember so much, when we want to. And they also ask how thinking works. They are actually no strangers to the world of thoughts, because they can see thoughts; but it is difficult for them to imagine how we can bring forth thoughts and ideas. They experience that we can handle thoughts and ideas freely.

That is an ability, however, that is unattainable for them. They experience how they are thought by higher beings, but are unable to think independently. However, they experience independent thinking through humans.

The elementals look up to human beings with respect and reverence. They are full of fondness for us; but at times they can also experience aversion toward us. They really look at what lives in a human being, not how he or she appears. The outer appearance means only very little to them. When they see that someone is full of deception or deceit, they turn away; yet when they see a developed personality, they feel an attraction. It is true that certain people cause a flight in the elemental world. Other people attract elementals and are constantly surrounded by them. In between these, all kinds of mixed types are found.

What do the elementals want of the human being? That question occupies me a great deal. Elemental beings gladly give an answer to this question.

> We are your sisters and brothers on a path of exaltation of the earth. Let us go together. Go with the earth, with its rhythms, its cycles, its tempo. The faces of the earth are your faces. It lives inside you; it lives outside you. It is much more to you than you surmise. It is more than your mother; it is also your father, your brother, and your sister. You can find everything, absolutely everything, in it.
>
> Its burdens, its sufferings are yours. Its joys, its happiness are yours. You are in no way separated from it. Only in so far as you have the ability to know it and to know yourself, are you separated from it. But that is all. Allow the separation to become a measure of your further development, but not a kind

of brutalization. Because the earth and its beings are in the process of becoming brutalized through what you plan and allow yourself to do, you are in the process of nourishing evil. It grows through the work of your beautiful hands. Unfortunately, it is so. We, however, see in every hand the hand it once was when it still belonged to a child. And we see in every hand the hand it will be when death has overcome the human being.

The time of development and change is always with us. That is why we can also see clearly the consequences of what occurs. We ask you to take our advice and try to work with the spiritual beings of the earth. They are there for you; they wish to instruct you and, together with you, they hope to form the earth to its highest potential. We can already see this future. We see the future and the life on earth, as it can be one day when people decide for this important cooperation with the earth and its beings.

To accomplish this, connect with others and speak about the future of the earth. A strong force of transformation and redemption can be released when you speak about the earth, about the germs of life that rest in the earth and want to unfold. The earth is a seed of the future that wants to germinate and grow, that wants to become big and fruitful. Only allow this possibility for development to exist. Try to be part of it, and try to see the secret life of the future earth.

Exchange thoughts among yourselves about what each one of you observes and sees; for many together always see more than the lone individual.

Individuals recognize much less the captivity in which they become entangled. But if they help each other to find, to see, to go the way to freedom, it very much lightens our work, which consists of freeing the soul from its imprisonment.

The earth has fallen into the state it is in, only because souls were imprisoned and lost the freedom to decide for themselves. Freedom is the key to saving the earth; freedom in an all-encompassing sense that does not exclude the innermost realms of the soul.

Therefore, go the inner path of development. But do not forget everyday life. Remember to beautify and enjoy daily life. Do not forget that pleasure must not be missing when one begins the earnest, inner path of development.

What you read here we whisper to you from the world we live in. We whisper this to you during the night in your sleep, but we also whisper it to you during the day when you are awake. Learn to pay attention to what we whisper to you from our world. You can learn only from what you hear, what reaches your souls from the secret sub-streams of life.

We ask you to surrender to a condition of sleeping-waking and waking-sleeping. Then you have an important key to hear and to understand us. Learn to dream into the appearances of life surrounding you. However, dream in such a way that you remain awake at the same time. Then your soul will arise with us, arise in our realm. Then we can be together and carry the earth in our hearts.

Through silence you come to us in our realm; in no other way. There is no other path except the one that leads through yourself. To begin with, learn to be fully present when you are quiet, or when you become silent. Penetrate your silence, learn to love it. Learn to love your silence as you love the light and its manifestations surrounding you. Penetrating your love for the light and its appearance during daily life is much easier than to penetrate your stillness of soul with love. And yet it is the field across which you must go to come to us. We will not let you have a choice.

As you see, there is the path that leads through yourself to the appearances of life. There is not only the path through the appearances to yourselves. There is also the other path, the path that leads into your innermost self and from there out again. It is a different language, which is connected with the path through you. You are not yet used to speaking this language, but you can learn this language that leads through you into the world, to the earth and its beings. It is essential for us, the beings of the elemental world, that you turn to that path and its language. We simply hear you better and more accurately when you speak in this language.

Lower your head, lower it to the earth. Lower it to where you perhaps do not assume that life, that beings, exist. Take your time for this until you have practiced placing your head itself into the earth. Your head has a true and deep relationship with the earth. Your head and the earth attract each other mutually; they are siblings. When you experience being siblings you have accomplished much and have understood it.

Begin to grow together inwardly with the earth. Your soul and your mind thirst for this union, thirst to research and experience union with the earth and with the appearances of life. But take up this research with your whole being. Avoid assuming that parts of you are not needed for this research. You are the best researcher about the concerns of the earth and for the earth, when you deal with yourself as a whole human being. Then you will serve yourself and the earth most successfully.

When you do this you will be rewarded. Try to feel the attitude toward knowledge that creates the greatest happiness and well-being in you. Learn to pay attention to what streams to you, perhaps on secret paths, from the objects of your studies. When you begin to learn and use the language that corresponds to the beings, then they can begin to be useful in your life. Make a great deal of observations in this sphere.

The earth is still, it is silent, as your soul is silent when it hears, when it listens, when it is deeply involved in learning, in perceiving, in broadening itself by this. Learn to know this condition of your soul, and learn to work with it. Strive toward it; let this soul condition of stillness, devotion, and listening become alive in you. Lose the fear of surrendering yourself when you enter into perception. You will not lose yourself, but find yourself, when you pass over into another being or condition and live in it. Only then will you come to know and recognize unimaginable new experiences, when you learn to listen out of the stillness of your soul. Then the earth will move through you, all the way through you. The separation falls away.

School of the Elemental Beings

It may sound strange, but there are beings of the elemental world who look at a human being and experience him or her as being in a kind of school, where they themselves are the teachers. There are indeed elemental beings who, in all modesty, experience themselves as teachers of humans. They desire to instruct us. It brings them great happiness when we allow them to teach us. Their instructions take place continuously and in many different ways. Mostly their efforts to connect with us go unnoticed. But their efforts nevertheless remain uninterrupted. It is justified to say that the beings of the elemental world court human beings. They yearn for nothing more than our listening to them, that we notice their advice, their signs and hints, and that we learn to read them. The school of the elementals into which humans enter as trainees consists of an uninterrupted stream of communication. This stream exists; but often it remains unnoticed.

The elemental beings have much to communicate to us. This is the case because they have rich experience with the living conditions of the earth. They have been on the earth already for a very long time. Many of them have seen innumerable generations of humans coming to the earth and going again.

The life of the elemental beings, however, is dependent on what human beings do, on what and how they think. Therefore, they have a great need, even a longing, to invite us into their school. They want to tell us that we need only take the signs of life, life's realities, seriously enough; that we need only consider with the soul what is shown to us in our daily life in order to recognize that we are in a school, the school of life.

It is not important that one be clairvoyant in order to be taught by elemental beings. All that is needed is the gift of exact observation. One must acquire the ability to observe exactly what happens. When one does this, one is able to recognize through it what the beings of the elemental world want to tell us. Elementals speak through signs, gestures, and moods. One needs a keen gift of observation to pay attention to what is so easily overlooked, to what appears as being of minor importance, or no importance, when one wishes to find access to the sign language of the beings of the elemental world.

Of course, the elemental beings are especially gifted in giving signs that belong uniquely to their area of activity. Through nature's moods, through the type and intensity of the wind and of the light, through cold and warmth, they make themselves known. Through the atmosphere of a place or of a period of time the elementals speak to humans. A refined attention in this area means that one awakens to the signals of the elemental world.

The beings of the elemental world are active not only where the visible world manifests, but also where every human being and every human community comes into contact with the sphere of their own destiny. Of course, the elemental beings do not have the power to bring about destiny; it is always higher beings that work through the sphere of the elemental world. They give the elemental beings the task of becoming active in the karma of an individual or a group of people. Seen in this way, elementals convey the karmic impulses that proceed from beings of higher worlds. They do this in a very concrete way. The elementals' sphere of life and the human sphere penetrate each other. Thus, elementals can become effective in the sense of the destiny of a human being. Therefore, everyday human occurrences and events belong to the elementals' realm of effectiveness.

It is important to understand this to get a picture of the effectiveness of the sign language of the elementals. Their signs are absolutely signs of destiny. Occurrences of importance always announce themselves through signs from their world. It can happen that suddenly a certain memory or an unusual thought arises. Or one becomes aware of a powerful feeling, or perhaps a premonition. Sometimes it is a wrong move or even an accident that is sent to us as an important sign; perhaps it occurred because elementals were involved in lowering our consciousness at a certain moment. Truly, many destiny-forming events occur because elementals work right into human consciousness. However, they never do this out of themselves, but always under a mandate from higher providence.

It is quite a substantial inner step to accept the fact that, as a human being, one is a pupil in this school of life. This insight is a kind of decision, a conscious deed that has to be accomplished over and over again.

The power of human consciousness is very important for the elemental beings. It is the prerequisite for them to cooperate with the human being. Elementals receive life forces through the consciousness of humans; this is a small but important secret. One might ask, what meaning does consciousness have for the surroundings in one's own life? What happens through my attentiveness? What happens when I accompany my doing and my perceptions with my consciousness? When one asks this question, one undertakes very decisive steps in the schooling which is spoken of here, for conscious deeds will always be answered in some way by the beings of the elemental world.

The power of human consciousness is of considerable importance for beings that penetrate, enliven, and create the earth spiritually. I am repeatedly surprised by the high respect elementals have for human consciousness. They talk about the fact that in the future the significance of human consciousness will increase even more. For the elementals, the strength that radiates from human consciousness belongs directly to life's reality, just as light belongs to our reality of life. Elementals are extremely sensitive to what human beings think and what they do with their attention. Often I could hear them say:

> Your thoughts are like bread for our life. We are nourished by what you carry and move in your consciousness. It is not intellectual thoughts that nourish us. We can build houses for our life from the streaming forces of thinking hearts. You feed on thoughts of the earth when you eat your bread; we are nourished by the thoughts that radiate from your hearts.

IV.
ELEMENTAL BEINGS AND HUMAN BEINGS

Border river at the Brocken between East and West Germany

House Spirits

House spirits are elemental beings that are very close to human beings. People are almost constantly surrounded by them. Yet, they are quiet spirits that do not draw attention to themselves. Their task demands that they adjust to the human way of life, so they act in a reserved manner with people.

But this does not mean that house spirits are weak spirits. On the contrary, they are strong and must be strong, especially because their life is so strongly interwoven with that of humans. Their closeness to people means that much is expected of them by human beings. They are chosen to share human destiny to a high degree. Living together with a human being is not always easy and enjoyable for them; it often exposes them to hard trials.

The house spirits receive insights into human life that no other class of elementals does. They see things that belong to the personal secrets of human life and are obligated to keep these to themselves. Guarding secrets is a virtue of these spirits. Nothing may be revealed of what human beings do and what they want to keep as their secrets. House spirits are forbidden to speak of something that the human beings they live with want to keep to themselves. There are other very communicative and talkative spirits among the elementals; there are even spirits who talk almost incessantly. These are important spirits because they see to it that no information that must be spread gets held up. They would not be suitable, however, as house spirits. It is precisely the silent way of house spirits that makes them close companions of humans.

This discretion of the house spirits expresses a basic feeling toward humans. They feel a great sympathy, yes, even love, toward the humans whose house, apartment, or room they share, and for whose guardianship they have been chosen. They are concerned for these human beings. They wish them only the best, and they wish that their charges develop in a way that is good for them.

It was a special experience for me to notice the attention a house spirit directs toward what a human needs for development. At first I thought they were beings that were not substantially different from other elementals that have tasks in natural occurrences of the earth. I thought that just as there are beings that guard a tree, a garden, or a landscape, so house spirits guard the house. But I noticed that this is not the case. One day I observed our house spirit next to the bed of one of our children. The child was sick and the house spirit had nestled close to the tiny body as if it wanted to warm it. It was quite worried and tried to help the child. I was deeply moved and realized that house spirits have tasks also in relation to the human beings who live together with them in the same house. On the one hand, they are connected with the house, as a tree spirit is connected with its tree, or a water being with a running stream; on the other hand, they look after the human beings who live in the house. That distinguishes them considerably from other elemental beings.

One morning when I sat in the room and meditated, I met my first house spirit. It sat next to me on the couch. It looked remarkably colorful and round. It looked at me with a radiant gaze, and was openly happy that I had noticed it. However, its gaze became immediately serious, very serious, and it imitated me as I was meditating. When I noticed that it was imitating me, I smiled, and we connected with one another. From then on it was there every morning, and it came when I began with my meditation. Soon it was ready for me to ask questions. Through it I learned many of the details about the life of elemental house spirits and their life together with humans.

House spirits are bound to the house; this means they cannot leave it. Just to go onto a balcony or a terrace requires that they overcome an inner resistance. They feel most comfortable inside the walls of the house. Within the house itself they can move unhindered through the walls from one place to another. This concerns above all the highest elementals of a house. In contrast to the spirits who have been assigned to a certain room or an apartment, they can move around the whole house. Their task is specifically to keep an overview of everything occurring in the house. At certain times when there is an unusual amount of activity going on in a house, they are forced to move back and forth between the different apartments. This is especially the case when they notice that there are difficult situations in several families at the same time. To accompany the families and the affected people is one of their main tasks. Whenever it comes to altercations or arguments, when problems have to be discussed, or when important decisions have to be made, they are present. They have the task of supporting the people in those situations. For them this is a very difficult duty. It is much easier for them to intervene in the destiny of human beings when they have been asked. Elementals of houses can be most effective for people when we want this; we can ask the spirits of the house to help us. A culture of mutual understanding is necessary so the house spirits can become active for humans. We have to make an effort to work together with the spirits of the house. What is meant by this culture of mutual understanding? What can we do for our house spirits? How can we enter into communication with them? Are there rituals that might help make it easier to live together with them? These are questions we shall concern ourselves with in the following.

As a first step it is important to acquire knowledge of the existence of house spirits and their circumstances of life. On the one hand, the house spirits are connected with the substances that belong to the house. They experience a deep connection with the material out of which a house has been built, and also with the substances that are carried into the house by the people. They also have a great interest in the processes of transformation humans put the substances through; for example, in cooking and eating. The things we carry into the house—food, clothing, technical gadgets—excite their attention. Because humans bring these things into the house, elemental beings can take part in events that happen outside of their own sphere of life. We human beings bring the world into the house for them through the things we bring with us. The house spirits need to look at these things in great detail. Therefore, I often hear the question, "What are you bringing with you? What do you have in your bag?"

But they not only look at the things, they also sniff everything. Things that we exhibit for them are examined, investigated, and admired from all sides. The house spirits examine things by fanning toward themselves the "air" that comes into the house with the goods, until they have had enough. They enjoy it when we bring things home from shopping and spread them out on the table, allowing them time to get to know everything.

A special elemental being lives in each room of an apartment or a house. They can look very different from each other. These room beings are very peculiar beings. They are not alone; they have a further host of beings around them that also live in the room, which are subservient to the room being. They are subordinate to the room being, just as the room being is subordinate to the house spirit. The spirit of the house is the being from whom the other spirits of the house slip out when they are needed. This is an event that takes place spiritually. In the same way, the room beings and the other ones slip back into the being of the house spirit when they withdraw from their connection with the physical world. They disappear into it as they have appeared out of it. It is therefore the mother being of all elementals connected with the house.

In addition to the room beings, there are in each room elementals that can be assigned to the four elements. In each room lives an earth being, a water being, an air being, and a fire being. When one wishes to clean a room, it is important that all four elements should be found in the corresponding ritual. One should have gifts for each element, so the beings that are connected to them may refresh themselves. Blossoms that one places into a dish with water and carries around while spraying the water are a refreshment for the beings of the air. The hefty scrubbing of the floor with water into which one has added flower essences refreshes the water beings. Burning wax candles and incense enlivens the fire spirits. One can awaken the earth spirits by knocking on the walls or by dispersing water and oil mixtures onto walls or floor. By reading certain verses to them, one can spread a feeling of well-being among them, which helps them free themselves from burdens they have had to encounter. They also love it when one sings to them. Also they react strongly to the inner presence of a human being. Just wishing to help them become lighter, more agile, and full of life is effective.

Every time, in the home in which we happen to be, we connect ourselves with what we are doing in such a way that we create a connection with the spiritual aspect of the earth, we foster the life forces of the spirits of the house. This can happen only if we fulfill the task we are doing with devotion. All deeds done with devotion are a source of life for the beings of the elemental world, and also for the house spirits. Whatever happens out of love nourishes the house spirits. Physical love is by no means excluded. Sexuality between people, when it is based on love, is a source of real happiness for the elementals. Elementals look intensively with admiration at people in love. For elementals, a couple in love is a wonder, just as the appearance of an angel would be to us. Also what happens between a mother and her children fascinates the elementals so much that they are almost unable to turn away. A nursing mother is always surrounded by many amazed elementals.

The spirits of the house wish that humans might become ever more conscious in handling the forces and abilities that they have. They do not love casualness, disorder, deceit, dishonesty or lies. Lazy people are a horror for them. When there is too much laziness around them, they themselves are taken over by it. One can observe that, in time, the house spirits take on the characteristics of the human being living in the house or in the apartment. This refers to all the character traits. They cannot really defend themselves against becoming like the people who are around them. One might interpret this as a weakness of the elementals. However, this is not so, for it is exactly their strength that they can adapt to human beings. The house spirits have dissolved their connection with nature in which many elemental beings live and have moved in with the human beings. They have connected themselves to human living conditions. They have dissolved their ties to the world of living nature, the trees, flowers, stones, brooks and rivers, the blowing winds; they have dissolved all these ties to serve human beings and to live together with them.

Just as every elemental being has received a task from higher spiritual beings, so too the life of house spirits together with humans is bound to a duty. The obligation of house spirits is to serve the development of humans. They have been singled out to serve the development of individual people. A house is there not only to provide a shelter and living space for its people. Through the house a space is created in which definite developmental steps take place. Seen in this way, to house spirits, a house is not a just a structure, but rather an extension of the skin of its human inhabitants.

The house spirits help to build this skin. They are spiritual beings through which a space arises that serves the individual and social development. The task that the house elementals have in relation to humans points to their high stage of development. They belong to the highly evolved elementals. For this reason they are highly regarded among the beings of the elemental world.

Every house has a house spirit. This also includes public buildings, schools, hospitals, concert halls; and also banks, factories, shops, and department stores. One can easily imagine that such beings have to be quite varied in their nature.

I had the opportunity to observe the house spirit of a school for curative education for a significant length of time. I could see how this school spirit greeted the children every morning by letting them walk through it. It placed itself in the entrance door in such a way that the children and youths had to walk through it. As they did this, it could feel them and this was its way to bless them. When an adult entered, it stepped aside. It was of the opinion that it would have to know whether the adults would wish to walk through it; if yes, it would stay. Its favorite place was, of course, the office of the school principal. It once told me with a mischievous grin that it was his great wish to have such a writing desk as the principal had. I must have looked astonished because it immediately explained by saying that its place was in reality at the table where all the children sit. But this is its heart. One can ask, what kind of table? It is an imagined table. This shows how deeply the house spirit is connected with the destiny of every child.

The school spirit knows the pupils, the boys and girls. It is even in a position to say something to individual children. When children are being discussed it is present; it listens carefully to what is being said about them. About the task it has, it once said:

It is my duty to guard the words that are spoken about the children, because these words have effects. When many people sit together and talk about a child, the effect of the words is especially strong. It is my task to protect the child from words that could harm it; and also to do everything I can that only words are spoken that are true of the child. But this is not an easy task. People could help a great deal to make this task less difficult for me. They would only have to imagine that the child is sitting among them while they talk. It is in fact the case that the child is there, only spiritually; however, only very few see this. But there is much more that you don't see.

Wandering Elemental Beings

There are highly evolved elemental beings that are not bound to a certain place on earth. Their lives consist of visiting the most varied places; they wander over the earth.

Some of these elemental beings move around in groups. I became conscious of these folk for the first time when I was hiking in the Engadin Valley in Switzerland. In front of the multitude of elemental beings marched a king. The king carried a crown and mantle, and led the crowd. They marched across my path and took no notice of me; apparently they were in a hurry to reach their goal. There was a troop of beings that were clad like soldiers. In between them were common folk. These beings did not wear modern clothes, but those of past times. Craftsmen and farmers were among them, and also women with children. I was very surprised. It was impossible for me to come into contact with them because soon they had disappeared among the trees. They seemed to have a definite path and mission.

Little folk of this kind wander everywhere on the earth, through its various landscapes, and even the cities. Doing this, they manage to go far, and they rest only briefly on their wanderings. They appear to be in a mad rush. Their mission is to reconnect whatever has been separated by human beings on the earth through their conscious or unconscious deeds. When somewhere in the world conflicts and altercations take place (wars are only their worst form), it causes ruptures in the elemental world. Through altercations that do not get settled, borders arise in the elemental world. This means that a severe argument between two neighbors leads to a boundary between the two properties that is insurmountable for many beings of the elemental world. The same occurs when there is strife between states or groups of states. Wherever borders of this kind appear, spiritual holes and ditches arise, which are hard for beings of the elemental world to bear. To resolve these is the task of the wandering elemental folk. Their appearance reminds one of earlier times, because they deal with forces that are likewise outdated and antiquated. They take on outwardly the form of the forces that they wish to overcome. They appear as a folk ruled by a king because the social and political arguments among humans arise from the fact that old lifestyles and attitudes still persist that should have been overcome long ago. These elementals turn the hierarchical social forms that are no longer timely into their own life form. They portray in their attire and through their behavior what they turn against. Their haste and their restlessness have to do with the necessity of overcoming the old conditions of life.

On the other hand, there are elementals that wander around on their own; they are lonely wanderers. They are closely connected with human destiny. They feel as if they would represent human beings among the elementals. They may never stay for long in one place, even if they want to. They feel strongly attracted to human beings and seek to be close to them in places where they stay. Through this they experience strongly how diminished the human faculty has become for being attentive to beings of the invisible worlds. People have turned away from the beings that are always around them, and through whom they receive the earth as it is. The wish to come together with humans is especially strong among the wandering elementals. For this reason they can be easily disappointed; they never appear hasty, but often seem sad and give the impression of being almost ashamed. These spirits are very quiet and unobtrusive. But it could also happen that they move around in groups. These groups, however, form spontaneously and continue only for a certain length of time. Even in their own community, every one of these beings remains on its own. When several come together they never move in bands, but always keep their distance from each other. In spite of that, they experience community with each other, but as a joining together of individual beings. When they come to a house, village, or a city, they observe people in detail. They try to find out where their help and support is most needed. When they have found a human being or a family, they stay with them for a certain length of time. It can even happen that they sleep next to the human being or in the same bed.

In the city one can find them in places where the homeless gather. They feel closely related to these people; they behold in them their own destiny. They accompany people who were struck by a heavy blow of destiny, or those who suffered an accident. They also go to people who actively support worthwhile projects; they are found in prisons, clinics, and in institutional homes. Even if they want to, they may not stay very long with one human being. After a certain time they have to move on. They do this so that they do not bind themselves too strongly to one person. This is because it is their task to become similar to humans; should they attach themselves to one person, they would run the risk of losing the individual traits they have already acquired. It would be a step backward for them to serve only one human being or one group of people. Therefore they are again and again sent on their way. Through this they arrive at an experience that is very unusual for elementals: they come to know loneliness. That is exactly their mission, as beings of the elemental world, to get to know the feeling of solitude. That is the reason they are attracted to people who are lonely, who are in situations in which they need to rely on themselves. They look for the lonely to come to understand solitude. It is precisely because they know loneliness, the feeling of being expelled, that they can comfort a human being.

A seminar that took place during the Holy Nights in Tessin, Switzerland, brought us unexpectedly close to those beings. Without really noticing it, we found ourselves in a group of such beings. It had already become dark, and many began to assemble as we made a fire in the forest. On the way back to the village the elementals accompanied us. They ran among us, which gave us the possibility to observe them closely. We could walk as they did, and experience the reason for their actions. These wandering elemental beings are young, youthful spirits. We were unable to tell if they belonged to a particular gender. They do not know death, and therefore have no fear. For this reason they appear extremely courageous. Yet we could experience that they were not free to decide on their path; they must go wherever they are called. Often they know their path only up to the step they are taking at that moment. For me it was an important experience to become aware of this. They actually never know whether they have reached their goal or not; they are always on the way. Of course, they know that they are guided, and they experience the guidance they are under.

These particular elemental beings love the community of humans. They love to be among people, to eat with them, to be present when they speak, laugh, sing, and celebrate festivals. Their favorite festivities, they said, are the birthdays of human beings. These communal gatherings that humans have are unknown to these elementals. They explain this by saying that they do not yet have the maturity to form communities as human beings do. Their wish for the human being:

> That you be more careful with the abilities that are yours. For us, you are often too loud and thoughtless. Therefore, we do not understand you. We understand you best when you yourself are clear about what happens in you and around you. The world of humans is strange to us. We learn slowly, but we learn also from the experience that each one of us has. We talk among ourselves about what each of us experiences. There are many magnificent moments we experience when we are allowed to wander among humans. Everything we experience is inscribed into us; imprinted not only into a single being, but into our collective consciousness. This type of consciousness is available to us because we are guided beings. We ourselves do not decide on our paths; the decisions are made for us. We carry out what other, higher beings have chosen for us. So our ways are not ours, but they become ours, as we walk them.

> The good fortune to meet you is completely on our side. We learn, and we learn much at every moment. When we are finished on the earth we transform ourselves. We return, die, if one can say that; but also we do not die, because we leave no physical sheath behind on the earth. We change into a new, different being when we die. So we are born anew; we arise among other spirits. As we

now wander in your world, we wander then among other beings and spirits. Where we will go we do not know; but we do know that every experience we have had among humans will be at our disposal in our next life. Nothing is lost. Absolutely nothing gets lost; everything will work further in some form. Everything changes; everything takes on a new form of life. Therefore, there is no death; there can be no death, no complete death.

The King of the Landscape

Elemental beings of the landscape are very numerous. It would be quite a separate task to describe all of them and their conditions of life. Quite early on, I met beings who are kings of the landscape, and through them I was able to gain much that is worthwhile. Originally, they belonged to the light and fire element; they are lofty, light-filled beings. On their head they wear an object that reminds one of a crown. Through it they indicate that they belong to a group of higher elemental beings. Their robes are elaborately decorated; colorful and varied forms have been worked into it. They are able to move around freely, yet they are bound to a certain place, which is their home. However, one can enter into contact with them even when one is not spending time in their locale. This shows that they possess a comprehensive consciousness.

Their being is connected with numerous aspects of the landscape. One of their most important tasks is to connect themselves to the life motives of those who have died. What continuously flows down from the realm of the dead into the life sphere of the earth is being incorporated into the elemental world through these beings. Through them the dead work onto the earth and within the conditions of the earth.

The value of this work should not be underestimated. There exists a life stream that continuously leads down from the souls of the dead to the earth and among people. Indeed, the earth could not appear in its radiating liveliness, as it does, if this stream of life did not exist. Through this life stream, the kings of the landscape receive their essential task: they serve the dead. It may be a strange idea that life forces from the dead stream down to the earth. The souls of the dead, after having gone a certain path after death, come into a condition that allows life forces to flow down to the earth from the realm in which they then are. They do this, of course, with the help of high spiritual beings. The kings of the landscape pass this life on to those elemental beings that are subordinate to them.

When one connects with the sphere in which the kings of the landscape exist, one connects with the souls of the dead and their realm. Through this one can come to experience how the earth should actually be treated. The dead have a great interest in the earth's being well cared for, because they need this planet for their following incarnations. Let us hear the words of a king of the landscape:

> Learn to know, O human, the consequences of your actions. To the beings of the elemental world, you are always active, regardless of whether you are asleep or waking. During the night when you sleep, we bear your sleeping soul through the landscape. Sleeping human souls go like large ships of clouds through the landscape. They go through our earthly bodily nature and unload among us what they have done during the day in their waking state. When they sleep they unload their freight among us in the landscape. They unload everything, the good and the bad; everything that moved the souls during

the day. Sometimes it happens that the nights set in like heavy thunder and storms. Fights humans have fought during the day take place during the night in the elemental world. Sometimes these storms rob us of the last confidence, the last faith in the good. There are times that are terrible for us.

However, at the same time, aside from the thunder, there is always the golden, melodious sound that sinks down out of the sleeping souls of human beings—as enchanting as the other is terrible. This too we come to see, and it puts us in a never-ending, forgiving mood when we can look into it. So much goodness, purity, and innocence lives in the souls of human beings. We look into them because they are part of our life substance; we receive nourishment from it. The light of the souls' purity continues to shine in us even when the souls have long gone on in their wandering through the realms of the night. Before the sleeping souls go into the sphere of the angels, they live among us. And then after they have been released from the sphere of the angels, they return through our realm, the realm of the earth, of the elementals, to awaken. The ascending and the returning souls go through our realm, through what the human being knows as the earth. Yes, so it is. There is this aspect of life, our existence, which has been let into your existence as an indispensable link.

There are many gifts that we, the beings of the elemental world, could present you with; these would come toward you if you could only grasp how you would have to transform your life. You would have to do it in such a way that we, the beings of invisible nature, could find a place among you in your hearts, in your sensing, in your interactions among each other. It is not difficult, it is not difficult at all; it is really not difficult. It is easy, it is very easy, extremely easy, and as easy as all that is, healing, binding, and uniting must be easy. Otherwise, it would just not be healing, binding, and uniting because there would be pressure, weight, and will involved, and far too much force. This is a sign of modern times, that humans employ too much power and are no longer used to making do with less. The helping spirits would gladly do their part; they would only have to get their place, the space, the permission to be able to work. It would mean that you begin to take elementals and the wonders and mysteries of life seriously. For strong forces rule in the world of the nature-spirits; they are the rulers and bearers of the forces of nature. The higher the rank a being has, the more forces it has available that can serve the human being.

It is not simply belief in elementals that shall return to the beings of the invisible earth their place among human beings. It will be human experience, knowing, exact knowledge, and the willingness to become a listening, attentive, observant, communicative and communication-receptive human being. However, humans can become this only because they already bear all of this within their innermost being. Don't be shocked by this sentence; it remains no secret to us beings of the elemental world what great capabilities exist among human beings on the earth. Tears come into our eyes when we consider the existing capabilities among humans. And tears come into our eyes because you use so few of them. You human beings could have created a different culture had you learned to use your spiritual capabilities better. You do not use them because you do not believe in them; because you have lost belief in what you are able to do, and in who you are. Belief in yourself and in the divine being you are was effectively driven out of you.

Human beings have great capacities at their disposal: the capability of empathy, faculties of intuition, and the capacity to feel the divine presence at every moment, in every being, in every cell. Light lives; streaming water sings; earth rings; air speaks; everything is; everything is being, is active. And all being in its own characteristic way can, for this reason, be experienced, felt, and described by a human being. So it is. Such is our view of things regarding the perceptive capabilities of the human being. In the sphere of morality the same is valid. An infinite amount has been accomplished by the hierarchies of the high and higher beings, so that the capacities for moral judgment and moral actions in human beings can live to such a high degree in our time, in these days and years.

Move across the earth with honest steps. The more you move truthfully and in a self-determined way, the easier our work of bearing the earth will be. For we bear the earth on the shoulders of our God-inwardness; and we truly love to bear the earth. O you human beings, because the earth has become too heavy for us, it would have to fall away from us if you do not take on whatever you are capable of bearing, out of the impetus of your own, strong initiative for truth. Otherwise, it will become cold on the earth and among you all. Your hearts will become cold if you do not come to know your capacity to carry the earth.

V.

CARING FOR THE EARTH

On the road between America and Europe

Care for the Earth

One can ask the question whether there are any means of supporting the beings of the elemental world in their work. This is an important question that is raised by many people in view of the situation in which the earth now finds itself. To start with, we need to have enough knowledge of what we want to care for and support. We need to know what kind of a relationship we have with the beings we want to care for. What relationship do humans actually have with the beings of the elemental world? How are we connected with this realm of beings? Suprasensory observation shows that during sleep we humans enter into a deep encounter with the beings of the elemental world. We do not necessarily know or surmise anything of this in our day consciousness, but when we are asleep, the soul, the part of our own being that detaches itself from the physical body, enters the elemental world.

During sleep, the soul of the human being expands. It ascends and is received by the high and the highest beings of the cosmos. On its way it passes through the elemental world, and the sleeping soul is received by the beings of the elemental world. The sleeping human soul then lives among the elemental beings for a certain length of time before moving on. The soul then enters the astral world and is received by the beings of that world.

The sleeping soul is received by those beings of the elemental world with whom it has met during its waking consciousness; it is attracted by the beings it has met during the day. The elemental beings take hold of the sleeping soul, envelop it, and lead it through their realm. The soul awakens among the beings of the elemental world to a consciousness through which it begins to connect itself with the spiritual life of the earth. These nightly meetings with the sleeping human souls are of important significance also for the elemental beings. Because they are visited by human souls, they can experience what their existence in the life of the human souls has caused. They experience what thoughts and feelings their presence has called forth in human beings. They experience these thoughts and feelings quite concretely. Through this they experience the effect they have on the soul being of humans. In this way a tree spirit experiences the thoughts and feelings its existence has caused in the human beings it has met.

These are the feelings of gratitude, astonishment, joy, and happiness one can experience through nature, and which penetrate during the night to the beings of the elemental world. Through these experiences of humans falling asleep, a kind of conversation occurs between people and the beings of the elemental world. To be sure, for humans this remains for the most part unconscious. In most cases no memory remains of this conversation, and yet such a conversation is not without consequences. They are confronted with a spiritual mirror by the elementals, through which they gain an impression of their relationship with the sphere of earthly life. From these nightly meetings with the beings of the elemental world, the soul takes away an essence, which it carries into its waking consciousness. Careful observation in the moment of waking up shows that a dim memory of this meeting is present. The soul learns something during sleep of the nature of the elemental world; its experiences in the elemental world reverberate on into waking consciousness. One can make it a habit to pay attention to these memories. They are essential impulses that we receive in this way. The elemental beings say the following to this:

Yes, we speak to humans! But you are not born with the ability to understand this language right away. Our language is a language like any other, in that one has to learn its words, its sentences, its sounds. But there it is, and there is not a human soul that does not receive it: as a lullaby, as soul language, as a rustling of soul-wind.

Gradually becoming aware of the experiences the sleeping soul has with the beings of the elemental world can be a step toward finding answers to the question about caring for the earth. Through the experiences we humans gain in this way, we can acquire an understanding of the spiritual connections existing between the elemental world and humans. We will be able to build up an intimate relationship with the spiritual beings around us. However, this personal relationship in no way requires that humans have suprasensory faculties at their disposal. It depends on individuals learning to build such a relationship out of themselves. It is really an individual decision to approach the beings of the elemental world; we humans can have a healing effect on the beings of the elemental world only of our own accord.

The elemental beings are always in need, but one cannot help them through impersonal methods of healing and caring for the earth. A prerequisite for the support of the work of the elementals is the accurate observation of the various processes and occurrences continuously taking place around human beings. Only in this way will we be able to find methods for caring for and healing the earth. It is really about acquiring an understanding for the living relationships that exist between human beings and the earth. Caring for the earth demands personal steps from those who know their responsibility for the earth. It is not about imitating what is right for other people; for the methods of others are theirs, which they have found for themselves. I am of the opinion that every one of us can find methods of our own for the caring and healing of the earth. We can be stimulated by other people, but that is all. We can assume that we ourselves have the imagination and the capabilities to start on a path on which we can support the beings of the elemental world.

The Body of the Earth

For the elemental beings, the earth is of special significance; it is the body they inhabit. Of course, not all elementals experience the entire earth. That is possible only for highly evolved elementals; and they are in this position only at a certain stage of development. However, even for highly evolved elementals this experience of the entire earth does not exist uninterrupted, but rather only for a certain length of time. They can encompass the entire earth with their consciousness only in special moments of their existence. These moments, however, are of great value for them; they carry these experiences with them like memories. The kings of the landscape whom one can encounter at special places are among these highly evolved elementals. Their consciousness extends across the entire earth. Spirits of old trees can also develop a similar consciousness. These elementals reach almost up to the world of the angels. The consciousness of lower-ranking elementals encompasses only a certain area of the earth. And yet they also experience the earth as their own bodily nature. They feel existentially bound up with the earth, just as we humans are existentially bound up with our own physical bodies.

Our becoming conscious of the importance of the earth for the elemental beings is not insignificant. The existential bond between the elementals and the earth with a certain place, a particular house, or a specific plant always exists.

When a change occurs in the earthly conditions it also means a change for the elementals. A wilting plant leads to a significant transformation in the life situation for the elemental beings of this plant. Intervention in the earthly conditions (for example, an excavation of a pit), existentially affects the elementals who live in that locality. The same goes for the felling of a tree, the building or demolishing of a house, and any activities of construction, even the plowing of a field. A change in the physical conditions of the earth always means an intervention in the structure the elementals live in.

Elemental beings are adversely affected, and even weakened, if they are not prepared in the right way for changes in their sphere. The fact that they are spiritual beings does not mean they are protected from physical changes. Therefore, they must be prepared for any changes that humans plan. It is always very important for them to be informed of what is planned; through this they receive the opportunity to adjust to a new situation and react appropriately.

The portrayed relationship of the elemental beings to the earth can give rise to certain considerations. When we wander through a landscape, through a forest, over a field, or walk through a city, we can awaken in ourselves a distinct feeling. We can awaken a feeling of being guests on the earth who find very definite living conditions here. These conditions, however, are brought about by the work of the beings of the elemental world. Their never-ending creating, their binding and releasing, the activity through which they conjure up life, accompany us every moment of our lives as we wander on the earth. We conduct our lives in a world in which we are guests. We need and use what these beings bring forth. Such thoughts can call forth a mood of gratitude in the soul. We can experience that by awakening to gratitude something significant occurs: we begin to enter into an exchange with the elemental world. Something like a subtle inkling of understanding begins to dawn.

The elemental beings perceive human beings. They experience our doing as well as our thinking. And they suffer when their guests do not accept what they offer with appropriate respect. Here, one can speak of true suffering. The elemental beings suffer pain when human beings react to gifts of the earth with ingratitude. They say:

> Your home is on our earth. The development of the earth goes through us, so that you receive at all times what you need for your development. We are your life. You live from us and through us. Every step, every word, and every soul gesture you owe to your life on earth. We are present in what you do and in what you leave undone. We accompany you and we also carry you, we penetrate you, and we watch over you. We lie in the garments of the great angels, which tower above the earth like stars, through which the stars can become visible, spiritually visible. We are the formable, spiritual-living substance of the great angels. When they speak, a stream of transformation goes through our world, and we ourselves take up the direction accordingly, as the needle of a compass is turned by the currents of the earth. But you too pass through us with every step you take. With every movement you make, with every word you speak, you penetrate through us and create something new that was never there before. We are the beings who adapt to what you do and think; in us is livingly imprinted your doing and your not doing.

Living Thinking

One can repeatedly hear from the elemental beings that humans trust far too little in the forces of their own consciousness. Elementals speak about the fact that we could heal the earth with these forces. Our consciousness has forces at its disposal that could help the threatened beings of the earth to overcome the pain, fear, and destructive powers through which they have been prevented from evolving further.

In attempting to understand this statement one is confronted with a mighty task. It has a weight that one would most happily avoid, but one becomes aware that it contains a profound truth. It is a great hope of the beings of the elemental world that human beings will acquaint themselves with this truth. The question arises, how should one do this? How can one grasp the forces of one's own consciousness? How can its healing force be experienced?

We want to try to come closer to these healing forces of human consciousness. A first step is to differentiate between living thinking and dead thinking. Living thinking derives from experience, from direct perception. Thoughts are linked to every perception. Just as the plant germinates from the seed, so are definite thoughts called forth by every perception. Dead thinking arises from completed ideas; the origin of dead thinking is ideas that are not experienced, but reproduced. The kind of imagining from which dead thinking arises denies the experience-character of ideas. It accepts an idea without experiencing it. For dead thinking, it is enough to understand ideas. To want to perceive and experience them lies beyond the conceivable. Living thinking unfolds exactly on this point. It takes hold of ideas by actively comprehending them. In this way it acquires experiences of those thoughts that provide the foundation for the ideas.

When one discovers living thinking, the need to subordinate oneself to an idea falls away. The need awakens to experience the ideas and to immerse oneself into the being of thoughts and ideas. Contemplating ideas in this way helps one come to one's own conclusions and decisions and to sharpen one's own ability to judge. Ideas exist to be examined; it is important to familiarize oneself with the ideas, but one should not feel pressured to become a slave to an idea. Being a slave to ideas does not originate with the ideas; it derives from an unwarrantable handling of them. Only through unjustified use do ideas become ideologies. Dead thinking is satisfied with the reproduction of thoughts and ideas; but living thinking wants to create thoughts. When one devotes oneself to thought life and learns to look at this as an independent being in itself, one will learn that one becomes capable of producing thoughts. Through this, one withdraws from all claims to power that can come from ideas.

Particularly today there exists a great danger of becoming a slave to ideas. The possibility lives in human beings to act out of their own intuitions. But that means to experience the living force that lies in thinking, which can provide access to the healing forces of consciousness. Healing forces can be developed only by a consciousness that arises from the life forces that slumber in the thought life. These life forces are the seed, the kernel of the transformative forces that are at the disposal of the human being.

Living thinking, and the forces that grow from it, present an immediate reality for particular elementals, similar perhaps to the flooding of sunlight for us. They experience the nourishing effect resulting from living thinking and the destructive effect resulting from dead thoughts. Living thoughts open a passage to the world of humans for the elementals. A bridge arises that unites what actually belongs together: human consciousness and the world of elementals. One can really see how certain elementals nourish themselves from the thoughts of humans. Certain thought forms appear to them like harmonious sounding, which leaves them uplifted and strengthened. One can say that elementals literally eat the thoughts that come from humans.

Steps toward Healing

How can human beings assist the beings of the elemental world? That is an important question we want to pursue in conclusion. It is important to consider that humanity cannot support, care for, or heal the beings of the elemental world by employing a particular healing method. Methods can serve only to help individual human beings find their own way to go forward. Methods may not be copied; otherwise, they become untrue. But they can point to possibilities of how one can proceed. They are not meant to restrict the individual person, but to expand possibilities. By studying methods of healing the earth, one can receive valuable suggestions about how one can refine one's own actions. However, one will have the experience that in cooperating with the beings of the elemental world it is also important to find one's own way, one's own method. The schooling one can experience from the elementals leads precisely to finding one's very own, original approach in working together with them. Every human being must find his or her own method.

Most important is the truthfulness of the acting human being. Does what we do coincide with our own personality, our own life's path? How much are we present in what we are doing? Do our actions, our talk, our thinking really come from us, or have we just adopted them because we thought perhaps it would be good, appropriate, or advantageous to act in this way? The elemental beings ask the human being:

What is the inner motive for your action? Why are

you doing what you do? Is it your own doing or that of someone else? This we ask you; and we ask you through the different life spheres of the earth, because we experience that untruthful action works like poison in our world. And truthful actions are like pure, liberating, healing light.

This may awaken an understanding for the healing forces human beings have at their disposal from the perspective of the beings of the elemental world. Therefore, it is important, when one accepts a task that serves the caring or even healing of the earth, to be clear about one's personal motives.

When we want to do something for a certain location because we realize that care is needed there, we should allow time to get to know the place well. The first step involves meeting the place with full awareness, including the beings who live there. For this, we need to allow time; under certain circumstances perhaps even a lot of time. The impressions we absorb must be able to resonate within us. When these impressions can resound in the soul of a human being, something essential occurs. We experience that the place begins to unfold its language, but only through the after-images in the soul. As observers, we can be so enchanted by the many details, through a first direct meeting with the place, that we can approach the most essential only with difficulty. We will find it easier to observe when we allow the accumulated impressions to resound in the soul. Through occupying ourselves inwardly with a place, we can distinguish the essential from the nonessential. The possibility of inner soul assessment of a place or landscape is much easier afterward. We have the experience that we behold not only with the senses, but also with the soul. In meeting a place both with concrete outer observation as well as with inner vision, we will notice how deeply we connect with it. A feeling of carrying the place within ourselves arises. We know it because we have inwardly experienced and seen it. The beings of the elemental world experience quite concretely how humans are connected with a place they live in. They feel the close or distant connection a human being has to his or her location. Outer and inner attentiveness are, therefore, the primary prerequisites for caring and healing work on the earth.

From the encounter that occurs between the human being and the beings of a place, the insights come for what can be done for the place. The spiritual beings of an area have requests for the human beings. If we dare to accept their requests, we will repeatedly meet smaller and greater surprises. Often their wishes are easily fulfilled. They may express a wish that one may return soon, or at least not forget the place, but let it live in one's soul. They may also express the wish that we should talk about our experiences with other people. These friendly, obliging ways are very meaningful for the beings of the elemental world. Through this the relationship between human beings and the beings of the elemental world is strengthened. One may also hear the following wish:

> Please do not forget what you have seen and felt here. Take it with you on your life's journey; and let it live again also in other places that you are led to. Through you the earth becomes a whole; through the paths you take on the earth, through your paths of destiny and the paths of your soul. When you walk in silence through a landscape, and your memories resound in you in a living way, the memories of places of the earth that live on in your soul, then you do much for the healing of the earth. In this way you give back from what you have received, and what you still receive hourly: the bearing force

and the trust of the earth and its beings in you. And you connect and unify the earth and its many places and landscapes. For it is no longer self-evident that they are connected. The earth ages; its ability to heal is limited; it has much and ever more to bear. Therefore, you have been asked to stand by its side with your inner strength of memory.

It would be a tremendous step forward if what has been expressed here in these few words would become a living experience among people. The forces for the healing of the earth are forces immediately available in everyday life. Healing is nothing extraordinary; rather, it begins where we humans use directly the forces at our disposal. So the faculty of memory is a healing force for the beings of the elemental world. But also the faculties of attentiveness, caring, and truthfulness are forces that serve the healing of the earth and its beings.

Again and again I am led to places that are obviously stressed. The elemental beings of such places often have only the wish that we simply stand still at such a place. These are places that are avoided, and where people look past them. But when we simply remain standing and look, we already do something quite unusual. There are many such places that really need this special attention and do not receive it. When we once stop at such an uncomfortable place and devote ourselves to what we can perceive there, we experience what it means to expose ourselves to darkness, to dullness, to emptiness and destruction. In time, we will get to know the forces living and revealing themselves in such places. These are definitely places from which we can learn a great deal. The darkness, untidiness, and filth are also instructive. I think it is very important to lose the shyness and apprehension to bear darkness. In this way we come to understand the situation of the elementals at such places. They are forced to bear the forces of destruction; they reveal them. By wishing to meet the beings who cannot flee from these places, but have to live there, we become aware of an important secret of the beings of the elemental world. We gain insight into the tasks they have in relation to evil. If we can bear to stand still at such places, we finally win the trust and respect of the elemental beings. They are astonished to meet a human being who, in spite of the destructive forces, proves that he has the unwavering steadfastness to remain. It is important only that we remain objective and do not give in to the hatred, fear, lethargy, and heaviness that can often be experienced at such burdened places. The more objective, calm, and loving one looks, the more welcome one will be to the elementals of these places. It is not a question of judging, but of bearing it. In this way one stands on the side of the beings of the elemental world, the beings that also guard such places.

Now I would still like to bring some requests I have heard from elemental beings at various places.

> Here is much dirt; take it with you.
>
> The creek is full of dead leaves; clear them away.
>
> Touch and caress the flowing water with your hand.
>
> Warm the cold stone with the warmth of your hand.
>
> Make a little fire and feed it with the wood of various trees.
>
> Put oil on the stones.
>
> Decorate the place with flower petals.
>
> Scatter flower petals in the water.
>
> Fill a small bowl with milk and put it there.
>
> Crush incense between stones and add it to the water.
>
> Kindle a fire; it gives us hope in the dark night.

Walk along there wherever your feet carry you.

Sing as you hear it sounding here.

Read something beautiful to us.

Make a fire on the stones in the river.

Create a beautiful form out of stones.

Take this stone with you—it has meaning.

Make a beautiful little place where we can once again breathe quietly.

Carry water from downstream and add it into the river upstream.

Play like a child with what you find.

Turn the stones.

Make a fire with a lot of smoke.

Set up a burning candle.

Write down what you hear.

Walk attentively.

Whoever wants to work together with the elemental beings must learn to listen to what reaches us from them. We should not, through wrong expectations, give a certain direction to what they want to communicate to us. Waiting without expectation can lead us when we want to get to know the requests the elementals want to communicate to us. They reward the attentive listener with gifts. They do this without making a fuss about it. Their gifts are modest but lasting, and they rarely correspond to our own imaginations or expectations. Therefore, the gifts, just as their originators, the beings of the elemental world, can be noticed only when we are attentive.

VI.
VERSES OF BLESSING

The orientation of life in the north

Blessing by a King of the Landscape for Human Beings

The Three Steps

Go slowly
  Back into yourself
    Feel the fullness of your own being
  You live
You are.

Open yourself
  Awake
    Bow to the beings
  That lovingly bear your life with you
Because the earth is your home.

Invite them
  To be life in your inner life
    To live in you
  As you live in yourself
To fill you as you fill yourself.

Then they will speak
  For they speak to you anyway
    But they want to be invited
      Otherwise they become silent
        When you look at them.

Verse of Blessing for the Elemental Beings

Thanking the existence
  Which bears the house of life
    I stand before you
  Spirits of the elements
Hear
  What human hearts
    Want to present to you
  Ships of happiness
Are sending
  Grateful hearts
    Creating life
  To you
Receive them
  Carrying them further
    Increasing
      Multiplying
    The deeds of love of humans
  Who would like to be
The earth's protectors.

By uniting itself
The life of the earth continues to work
To help so that the spirits
Come together,
The human spirits

And the earth spirits
Uniting in a strong bond
Which receives
New life.

Help to bear
  What humans already bear
    Who wish
  To transform the earth's suffering
So that new can arise from the new
  Without pause
    The law of life
  Continues to live
In everything.

Go with those
Who already walk
On whose shoulders
In whose hands and hearts
The earth already is
Their child
That they protect
As a mother
Protects life
That out of her
Arose.

So can the new become new

For in the beings of the elements
Works

Life of higher world beings.
The elemental spirits are
This higher life's
Living image.

With this life the soul unites
That understands the senses' veil
As flooding work of the spirit.
Let me belong to the life
Speaking through you
Teach me to read
Teach me to behold
Teach me to understand

And take me by the hand.

Chorus of the Elemental Beings

In your hands rests
  The life of the earth.
In your souls
  Give it the right to live
    As is fitting for it.
    Then it cannot fall
  Which falls so easily,
For it is old,
  But young
It remains through you.

Karsten Massei

Karsten Massei was born in 1963 in Berlin. He started out by studying political science, but then decided to train in Switzerland as a curative educator. He is now a class teacher in a curative day school and also gives courses and seminars on the practice of suprasensible perception and leads tours that are focused on the experience of and care for the many different kinds of landscapes and life spaces of the earth. In addition, he is active with biographical and life counseling and supports therapists with advice about their work. He lives in Zürich.

About the illustrations by Franziska van der Geest

Franziska van der Geest was born in 1959 in Basel, Switzerland. Since her childhood she has engaged in intensive contact with nature beings and beings of the higher hierarchies. This enables her, on the one hand, to have deep knowledge of the many-sided connections in the sphere of life. On the other hand, out of this developed extensive biographical and business counselling work.

Since 2001 she has traveled extensively through Europe and the Americas. These journeys are dedicated to the research of the spiritual geography of landscapes and to the healing of the earth.

During her travels, Franziska paints. In her paintings, in which she captures the astral and etheric movements related to places and landscapes, the suprasensory happenings there become visible. The wishes of the beings connected with each respective location are expressed. The pictures contain messages for human beings. Above all, these are beings of the elemental world that support the process of painting. On the paper, colored lines and forms are shown to her, which she then draws and paints. Over the years, a rich and varied work has come into being in this way.